Data Design

Bloomsbury Visual Arts
An imprint of Bloomsbury Publishing Plc

Imprint previously known as A&C Black Visual Arts

50 Bedford Square
London
WC1B 3DP
UK

1385 Broadway
New York
NY 10018
USA

www.bloomsbury.com

British Library Cataloguing-in-Publication Data
A catalogue record for this book is available from the British Library.

ISBN HB: 978-1-4081-9188-0
PB: 978-1-4081-9187-3

Library of Congress Cataloging-in-Publication Data
Mollerup, Per
Data Design: Visualising quantities, locations, connections / Per Mollerup p.cm
Includes bibliographic references and index.
ISBN 978-1-4081-9188-0 (hardcover) ISBN 978-1-4081-9187-3 (pbk.)
2012045678

Design by Per Mollerup
Printed and bound in China

Data Design

Visualising quantities, locations, connections

B L O O M S B U R Y

LONDON · NEW DELHI · NEW YORK · SYDNEY

Contents

As knowledge increases amongst mankind, and transactions multiply, it becomes more and more desirable to abbreviate and facilitate the modes of conveying information from one person to another, and from one individual to many.

William Playfair

The Commercial and Political Atlas, 1786, *pVII*

Introduction

Organising knowledge

Data Design deals with data visualisation to organise knowledge about the world into charts, maps, and diagrams. Data visualisation makes raw data useful. This book is not about data decoration.

Data visualisation constitutes a branch of information graphics, which in turn provides visual explanation in fields as diverse as document design, wayshowing, human–machine communication, and interaction design.

Data visualisation reorganises data, presenting it in ways that answer relevant questions by making data easily perceptible and comprehensible. It domesticates raw data to make it clear and usable as a basis for decisions.

The three subject categories in this book – quantities, locations, and connections – are visualised in different, yet similar ways. Together with hybrid forms, the similarity suggests a parallel discussion, although in separate parts.

Data Design is written and designed to assist designers, researchers, and writers to express visually what can better be explained and understood by position, shape, size, and colour than by words, letters, and numbers. It describes problems, principles, and solutions for the visual display of information, and it presents didactic examples from the real world.

Data Design concentrates on the principles of data visualisation. The choice of computer, software, and type of coding are up to the reader. Such fast-changing aspects of data design will develop into something different from today's versions in the near future. When they do, the principles in *Data Design* will still be valid.

First, *Data Design* discusses the theory behind visual displays and presents basic principles. Second, *Data Design* presents an array of well-known and lesser-known display formats. Together, these principles and practices will enable readers to make useful and engaging visual displays off the rack, along with possible new forms of data design.

Per Mollerup
Melbourne and Copenhagen, 2014

Most captions in *Data Design* are placed a short distance from the illustrations they explain. When learning about the law of proximity, readers might wonder why. There are two reasons for this apparent failure to obey our own laws. The first reason is purely didactic. Separating illustrations and captions gives readers a chance to see and understand the intentionally self-explanatory charts, maps, and diagrams undisturbed. The second reason is that it adds to the sense of order, ensuring that the displays are not embraced by words.

The text of some of the imported visual displays in *Data Design* is difficult to read. The book format and the resolution of the illustrations don't allow bigger illustrations. While text in displays should normally be perfectly readable, readability of the display text is less important in *Data Design* since it is the principles that matter.

Field of study

Goals

However different in its visual results, data visualisation shares goals with writing. When we write, we do so with one or more of three goals in mind.

Communicate

First, we write to communicate: to share thoughts, information, and desires with others. In a certain sense, this is the most demanding goal of writing, as it involves the receiver's perception and cognition. The latter implies that the sender and receiver of communication share a code. For researchers, writing to communicate is important in so far as we require good research to be accessible to others.

Record

The second goal of writing is to record what otherwise might be forgotten. This is our goal when we keep a log or diary, produce a list of things to do, write an aide-memoire, or prepare a manuscript for a speech.

Understand

The third goal of writing is the most interesting, particularly to researchers. We write to understand. Serious writing is a conversation with the person we know better than anybody else: ourselves. Seeing our thoughts on paper helps us to improve these thoughts and inspires us to think new thoughts. Many of us would not be able to think as well as we do without writing, and without reading what we write.

Data visualisation serves the same three goals as writing: to communicate, to record, and to understand, with the emphasis on communicating and understanding.

Field of study

Benefits

It takes energy, thought, and time to make good visual displays that can substitute for stacks of naked numbers and lengthy verbal descriptions. These human and economic costs can be justified by at least four benefits:

– *Understandability*

Visual displays present qualitative and quantitative relationships in ways that are easier and faster to understand than text and numbers alone. A written explanation of the connections between London's 270 Underground stations would take 72,630 (270x269) individual explanations; even more with alternative routes. The iconic Tube map *(see p21)* provides all this information on a single sheet in a pocket-sized format. Most importantly, the map is easily accessible to users.

– *Insight*

Visual displays reveal relationships and trends that may be difficult to see when the subject matter is explained only in words, letters, and figures.

Figure 1 Many visual displays designed for fast comparison are supplemented with numbers to offer exact comparison. These displays use the best of both worlds: the speed of visual displays and the exactness of figures. They are hybrids between visual displays and tables. The visual part of this horizontal bar chart shows the growth of US national debt in absolute terms, while the figures also show that the growing debt is decreasing compared with the GDP.
Data and design concept sourced from *USA Today*, USA, 21 Sep 2011

Figure 2 This Dorling cartogram shows the nations of the world as circles sized according to the charity-giving of the population. The map is able to tell us faster than a table would be able to which nations are the most charitable and how a specific nation ranks.
CAF World Giving Index 2012, Charities Aid Foundation. Available from www.cafonline.org/pdf/WorldGivingIndexA3Map2012WEB.pdf

Living within means?

Even if recommendations President Obama made Monday are enacted, the national debt would increase $6 trillion over the next decade.

Year	National debt held by the public (in trillions)	Debt as a percentage of GDP
2012	$11.7	74.6%
2013	$12.7	76.9%
2014	$13.3	76.4%
2015	$14.0	75.9%
2016	$14.7	75.6%
2017	$15.3	74.3%
2018	$15.9	74.2%
2019	$16.5	73.8%
2020	$17.1	73.4%
2021	$17.8	73.0%

1

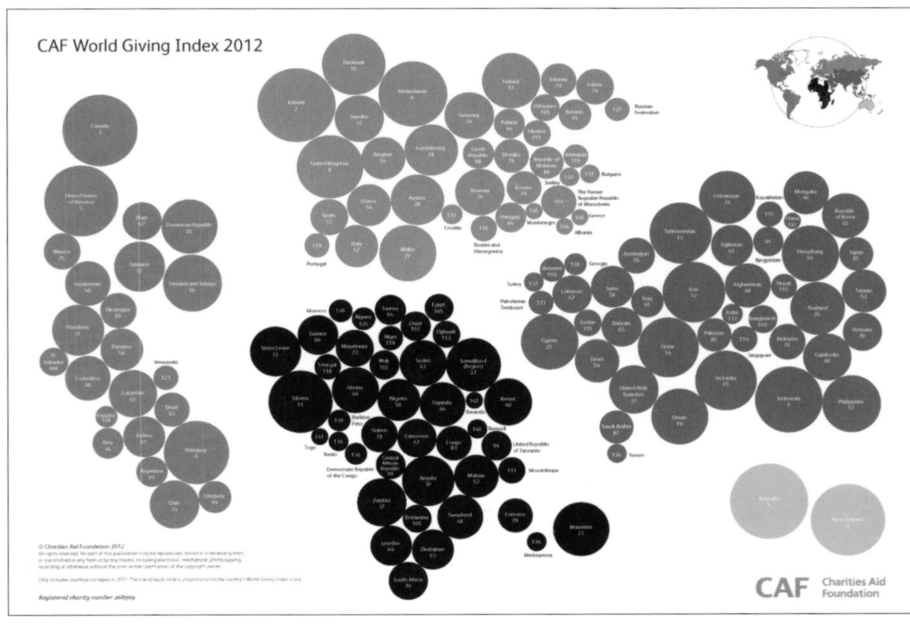

2

– *Attention*
Well-crafted visual displays capture and hold the attention of the audience. Capturing attention is a legitimate reason for data visualisation. In principle, researchers choose visual displays for understandability and insight. Media editors frequently choose visual displays to invigorate their products.

– *Memorability*
Simplicity and elegance can make visual displays more memorable than other means of expression. "To remember simplified pictures is better than to forget accurate numbers," as stated by Otto Neurath, the creator of Isotype *(see p30)*.

The first two benefits, understandability and insight, deal with the way the reader understands the subject matter; the last two benefits, attention and memorability, deal with the way the visual displays impact on the reader's scarce attention and memory. Different situations call for different combinations of these benefits.

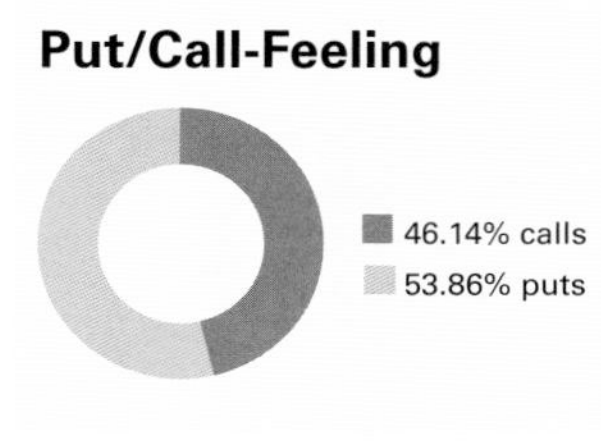

3

Figure 3 Donut chart as seen in *Neue Zürcher Zeitung*, the well-known Swiss newspaper.
The role of the donut chart on a page filled with text on financial matters is to draw the reader's attention to the fact that the market is slightly less optimistic (calls) than pessimistic (puts). The figures need no explanation.
Data and design concept sourced from *Neue Zürcher Zeitung*, CH, 21 Sep 2011

To remember simplified pictures is better than to forget accurate numbers.

Otto Neurath

Empiricism and Sociology, 1933/1973, *p220*

Field of study
Information graphics

Data visualisation constitutes a branch of information graphics, a term which is not totally precise. Taken literally, information graphics include all kinds of graphic design, but the commonly used restricted sense of the term designates a specific type of graphic design that works with objectivity and clarity of expression.

– *Definition*
IIID – the International Institute for Information Design – defines information design as

> 'The defining of the requirements governing the selecting, rendering, and transmission of information for the purpose of knowledge transfer as well as the optimisation of the information with respect to these requirements.'

While this definition can, in principle, include disciplines other than visual design, we shall concentrate on graphic design. For clarity, we can define information graphics as the

> design of visual explanation

where the term *design* covers the design process as well as the result of that process.

"A definition will often be more comprehensible for being made longer, but any gain in precision tends to be offset by the reader's resulting muddlement."
Henry Hitchings
Dr Johnson's Dictionary, John Murray, London, 2005, p81

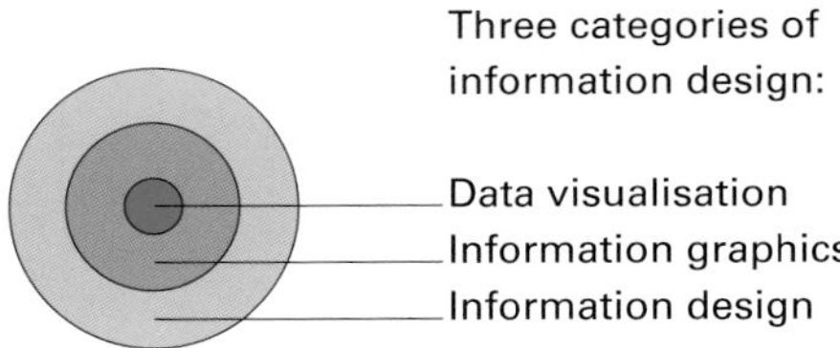

– *Problems addressed*
Information graphics typically deal with issues that are both complex and complicated. Complex means consisting of many interrelated elements. Complicated means difficult to understand or analyse. Complexity often results in complication. Complexity is an objective quality, it deals with facts; complication is a subjective quality, it depends on the reader's perceptive and cognitive capacities. What is complicated to one reader may be simple to another. The word *reader* is here used synonymously with *receiver*.

– *Outcomes*
Information graphics are descriptive, or prescriptive, or both. Descriptive information presents the facts of the world. For example, a line chart showing the development of a nation's export is descriptive. It deals with knowledge and enables sense making. Prescriptive information tells the receiver what to do. For example, user instructions are prescriptive. Prescriptive information deals with action and suggests following rules.

The boundary between description and prescription is not always sharp. Two signs, one saying *Staff only* and the other *Do not enter*, present basically the same information, but are categorised respectively as description and prescription. A single geographic map can offer both a general description of an area and give special route information, telling readers how to get from A to B. The displays presented in *Data Design* are – with very few exceptions – descriptive.

– *Objectivity*

Information graphics are intentionally objective. The information describes facts not coloured by the feelings of the sender, and addresses the understanding rather than the feelings of the reader. It can be argued that all information graphics are subjective to some degree, since humans design them. However, information designers consciously strive to make information as objective as possible.

Information graphics are concerned with information located in two of the six content fields in the information matrix* below: objective prescription and objective description. Data visualisation deals primarily with objective description (the result – visual displays – is printed in bold in the matrix).

*Inspired by Pierre Guiraud *Semiology*, Routledge, London, 1975

Six categories of information – with examples			
Category >	Identification	Prescription	Description
Objective >	ID number	User instructions	**Visual displays**
Subjective >	Clothing	Advertisement	Painting

– *Clarity*

Clarity is key to good information graphics, which are intentionally unambiguous, corresponding to what Umberto Eco describes as *closed text*: not open to free interpretation.

– *Language*

As a graphic design discipline, the field of information graphics is concerned with visual representation of facts by definition. Nevertheless, language plays an integrated role in many kinds of information graphics, notably document design. Plain language is a special discipline that strives to make language accessible to as many readers as possible.

– *Fields of application*

The field of information graphics is sometimes divided into document design, human–machine communication, and wayshowing. Information graphics, however, deal with a larger number of visual communication issues, including:

- Cartography
- Data visualisation
- Document design
- Financial information
- Interactive design
- Human–machine communication
- Medical information
- News graphics
- Product graphics
- Road signs
- Slide presentations
- Technical illustration
- Traffic and transport information
- Timetables
- User instructions
- Warning signs
- Wayshowing
- Web design

– *Elegant efficiency*
Good information graphics are factual, objective, and unambiguous. They are also elegant. This means that they are beautiful, simple, and effective. In the same way that mathematicians discuss elegant solutions and engineers construct elegant bridges, designers of information graphics should design elegant charts, maps, diagrams, and other outcomes.

Information graphics don't have *one* optimal solution determined down to the last pixel by a technical formula. Once the technical demands are met, there is always space for an elegant solution. Information graphics should encourage intended readers to take a closer look. Even so, this is not a licence to create overly smart information graphics that need to be explained themselves rather than explaining something.

Just as some architects today consider architecture primarily a question of artistic expression and consider function a secondary necessity, some graphic designers prioritise artistic displays with little concern for perception and cognition. *Data Design* does not take this approach.

Understanding means simplifying, reducing a vast amount of data to the small number of categories of information that we are capable of taking into account in dealing with a given problem.

Jacques Bertin

Semiology of Graphics, 1983, *pIX*

Field of study

Simplicity

Most of us today suffer from cognitive overload. We feel that we are offered too much information, which is too poorly organised. The amount of information we feel we must know and understand wildly surpasses our available time and capacity. Some experts hold that this state of affairs is due to filter failure. No matter what, those who send messages should strive for simplicity to capture and hold the attention of their intended audience. Good visual displays simplify information in terms of quantity and, especially, quality.

Complexity is part of the modern human context. If we want to reap the benefits of the modern society, complexity will remain an intrinsic part of our situation. Most often, complexity causes complication. No matter how well designed it is, the elegant but complex map of the London Underground is more complicated than the map of the smaller and less complex Copenhagen Metro.

Figure 4 Transit map: London Underground. 270 stations, 11 Underground lines, plus DLR Docklands Light Railway and National Rail. Courtesy of London Underground Map, TfL

Figure 5 Transit map: Metro, Copenhagen. 22 stations, 2 lines. Courtesy of Metro, Copenhagen

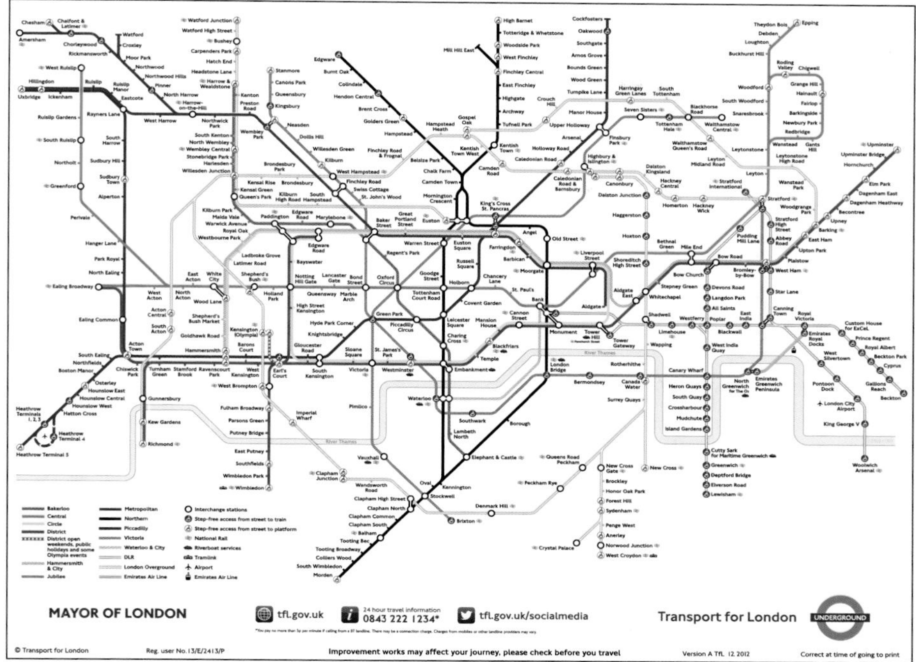

MAYOR OF LONDON
tfl.gov.uk
24 hour travel information
0843 222 1234*
tfl.gov.uk/socialmedia
Transport for London
UNDERGROUND
© Transport for London
Reg. user No. 13/E/2413/P
Improvement works may affect your journey, please check before you travel
Version A TfL 12.2012
Correct at time of going to print

4

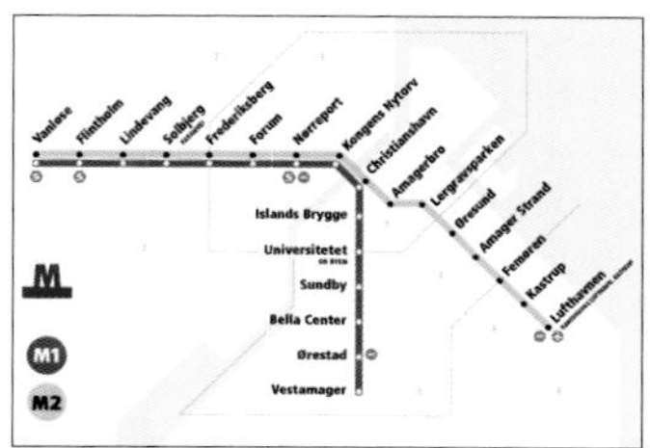

Vanløse
Flintholm
Lindevang
Frederiksberg
Forum
Nørreport
Kongens Nytorv
Christianshavn
Amagerbro
Lergravsparken
Øresund
Amager Strand
Femøren
Kastrup
Lufthavnen
Islands Brygge
Universitetet
Sundby
Bella Center
Ørestad
Vestamager
M
M1
M2

5

Field of study

Milestones

Today, data visualisation formats are the result of a long development. Visual displays representing quantities, locations, and connections are not a recent invention.

– *Describing the world*

Man has probably always felt an urge to describe the part of the Earth's surface he thinks he knows. Exactly when cartography was born is debatable, but it was well before the Christian Era (CE). The history of cartography offers many highlights. One is the T-O map, another is *Theatrum Orbis Terrarum,* Theatre of the World.

Fifteenth-century T-O maps are strongly simplified displays of the world: maps for understanding the big picture rather than for wayfinding. T-O or O-T stands for *orbis terrarum*, circle of land. The maps show the temperate part of the world: Asia, Europe, and Africa divided by the T: the Mediterranean, the Nile, and the Don. The O is the encircling ocean.

Theatrum Orbis Terrarum by Flemish cartographer and geographer Abraham Ortelius (1527–1598) was first published in 1570 in Antwerp and is considered the world's first modern atlas: a book of map sheets with explanatory text. However beautiful, the maps of *Theatrum* are not up to contemporary standards. Inaccuracies are understandable, given the publication date. Less understandable in our day is the inclusion of fantasy elements such as several non-existent islands in the map of the North Atlantic Sea: Brazil, Frieslandt, and Grocklandt.

Figure 6 T-O map by Günther Zainer, 1472. T-O maps simplify and categorise rather than show the way. The three land parts were considered the domains of the three sons of Noah: Sem, Iafeth, and Cham.

Figure 7 The North Atlantic Sea. *Theatrum Orbis Terrarum,* Theatre of the World, by Abraham Ortelius, 1570. The world's first modern atlas is characterised by beauty, fantasy, and imprecision compared with contemporary maps.

Oriens
MARE OCEANVM
ASIA
Sem
Mare magnum siue
EVROPA
Iafeth
mediterraneum
AFRICA
Cham
Septentrio
Meridies
Occidens

6

SEPTENTRIO
AMERICAE SIVE NOVI ORBIS PARS
Groenlandt
Estotilant
OCEANVS HYPERBOREVS
MARE CONGELATVM
Pigmei hic habitant
Islant
OCEANVS DEVCALIDONIVS
OCEANVS OCCIDENTALIS
OCCIDENS
RVSSIA
ORIENS
SVEDIA
Liuoniæ pars
Biarmia
Hebudes insulæ
OCEANVS GERMANICVS
Oostsee
Prussiæ pars
Pomeraniæ pars
OCEANVS BRITANNICVS
MERIDIES
SEPTENTRIONALIVM REGIONVM DESCRIP.

7

– *Time made visible*
Thinking of time as a line is an old practice. However, it was only in the middle of the eighteenth century that visualising time as a line going horizontally from left to right was introduced. In his book, *Chart of Biography,* 1765, British scientist and theologian Charles Priestley (1733–1804) introduced this timeline format to mark the births and deaths of famous historic people. The decisive difference between Priestley's timelines and early chronographic tables is overview. Priestley's predecessors used vertical tables with the earliest time at the top and the latest time below. These tables are less effective when it comes to overall reading. Horizontal timelines give the temporal details and present the overall picture as well.

After the Crimean war (1853–1856), Florence Nightingale (1820–1910) developed a polar chart to show the true causes of death month after month: primarily bad hygiene rather than wounds. The length of the slices of the 12 equiangular wedges represents the number of casualties. The polar chart can be considered a special version of the radar chart *(see p98).*

Figure 8 *A New Chart of History,* timeline by Charles Priestley, 1769

Figure 9 *Diagram of the causes of mortality in the army in the East,* polar chart by Florence Nightingale, 1858. Red stands for death from wounds, blue for death from bad hygiene, and black for other causes.

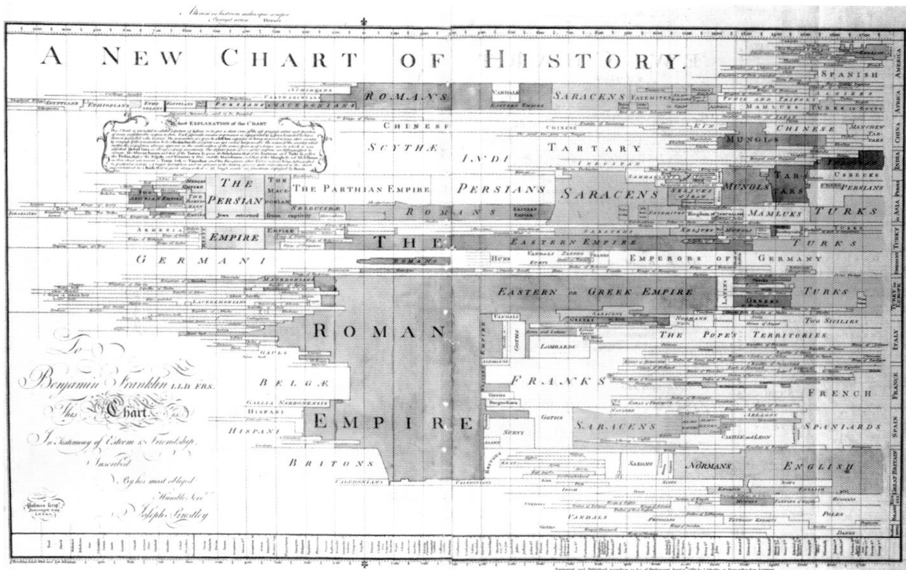
A NEW CHART OF HISTORY.
ROMANS
CHINESE
SCYTHÆ
INDI
TARTARY
THE PERSIAN EMPIRE
THE PARTHIAN EMPIRE
PERSIANS
SARACENS
MUNGLS
TURKS
SPANISH
GERMANI
EMPERORS OF GERMANY
EASTERN or GREEK EMPIRE
ROMAN EMPIRE
THE POPE'S TERRITORIES
FRANKS
FRENCH
SPANIARDS
BRITONS
NORMANS
ENGLISH
To Benjamin Franklin LL.D. F.R.S. This Chart is in Testimony of Esteem & Friendship, Inscribed By his most obliged Humble Serv.t Joseph Priestley

8

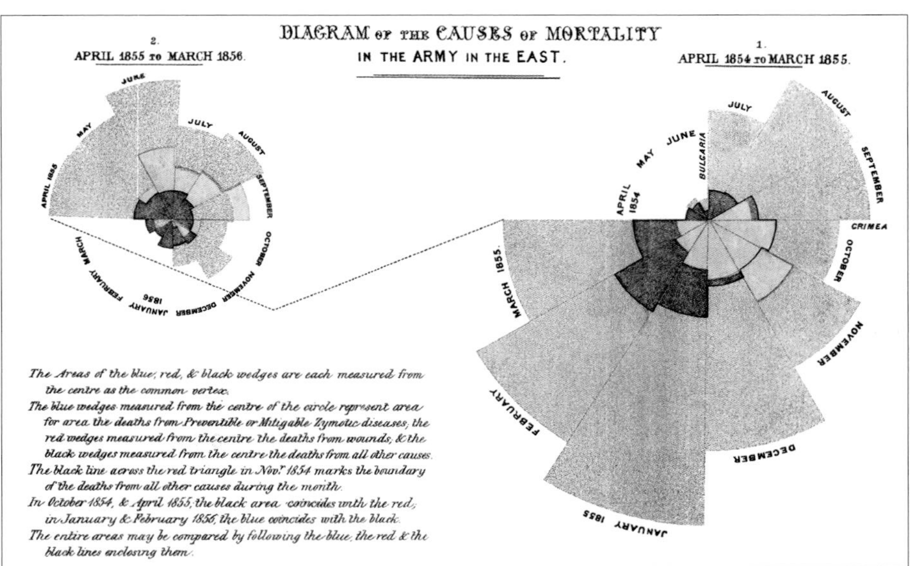
DIAGRAM OF THE CAUSES OF MORTALITY
IN THE ARMY IN THE EAST.
2.
APRIL 1855 TO MARCH 1856.
1.
APRIL 1854 TO MARCH 1855.
APRIL 1855
MAY
JUNE
JULY
AUGUST
SEPTEMBER
OCTOBER
NOVEMBER
DECEMBER
JANUARY 1856
FEBRUARY
MARCH
APRIL 1854
MAY
JUNE
BULGARIA
JULY
AUGUST
SEPTEMBER
CRIMEA
OCTOBER
NOVEMBER
DECEMBER
JANUARY 1855
FEBRUARY
MARCH 1855.
The Areas of the blue, red, & black wedges are each measured from the centre as the common vertex.
The blue wedges measured from the centre of the circle represent area for area the deaths from Preventible or Mitigable Zymotic diseases; the red wedges measured from the centre the deaths from wounds; & the black wedges measured from the centre the deaths from all other causes.
The black line across the red triangle in Nov.r 1854 marks the boundary of the deaths from all other causes during the month.
In October 1854, & April 1855, the black area coincides with the red; in January & February 1856, the blue coincides with the black.
The entire areas may be compared by following the blue, the red & the black lines enclosing them.

9

– *Space and time*

One of the most famous visual displays ever made is probably *Carte Figurative des pertes successives en hommes de l'Armée Française dans la campagne de Russe 1812–1813,* a visual display of the losses of the French army during the Russian campaign of 1812–1813 by Charles Joseph Minard (1781–1870).

This map has three variables that concurrently show the army's location and movement, the army's declining size, and the increasingly low temperatures during the retreat, all in an inherent timeline. The timeline has two directions, one for the French invasion of Russia and one for the retreat. The retreat and the temperatures during the retreat should be read from right to left.

Overall reading of the thickness of the line that stands for the ever-decreasing number of troops is evidence of the catastrophic war. A one-way timeline is preferable for most practical purposes.

Figure 10 The losses of the French army during the Russian campaign 1812–1813.
Map by Charles Joseph Minard, 1861

Figure 11 Part of figure 10 enlarged and redrawn to show details.

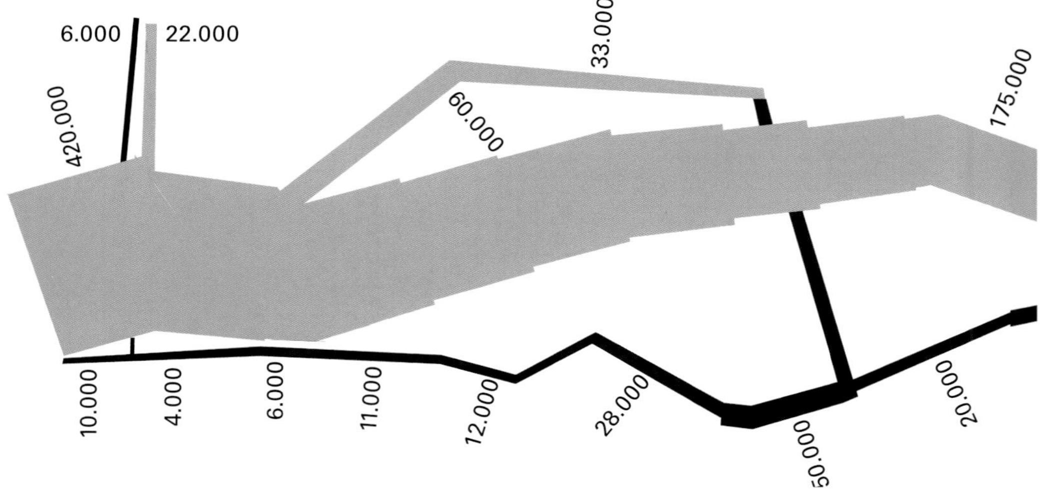

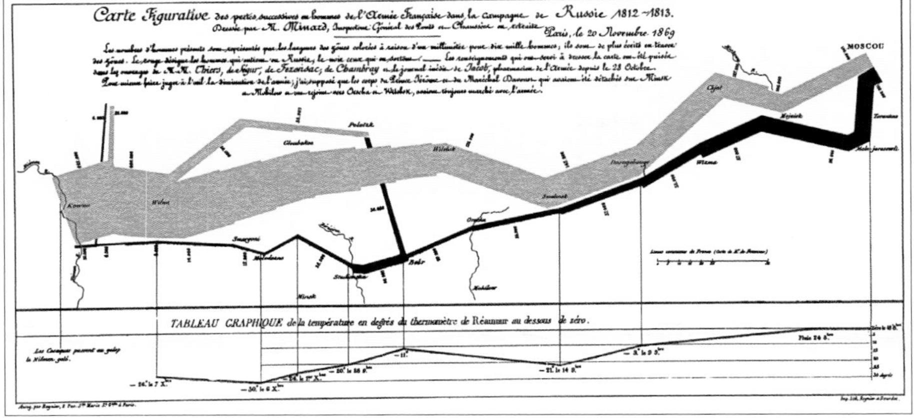
Carte Figurative des pertes successives en hommes de l'Armée Française dans la campagne de Russie 1812–1813.
Paris, le 20 Novembre 1869
MOSCOU
TABLEAU GRAPHIQUE de la température en degrés du thermomètre de Réaumur au dessous de zéro.

10

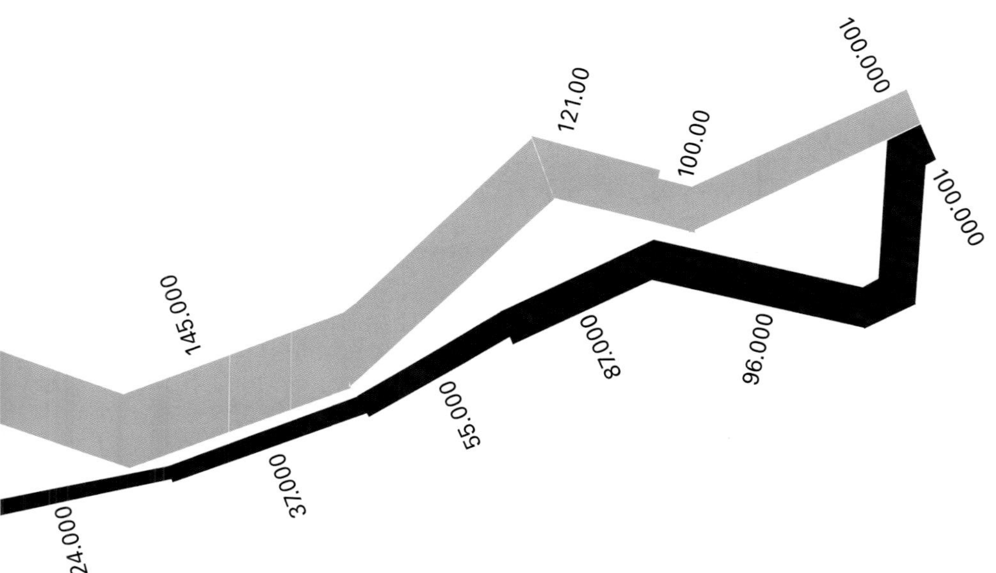
100.000
121.00
100.00
100.000
145.000
87.000
96.000
55.000
37.000
24.000

11

– *Visualising quantities*

William Playfair (1759–1823), a Scottish engineer and political economist, showed the world that abstract visual displays are superior to tables in certain respects. Playfair invented three of the types of visual display most frequently used for quantitative information today.

Over two hundred years ago, Playfair presented the world's first line charts and the first bar chart in *The Commercial and Political Atlas* (1786). He presented what is considered to be the world's first pie chart in *Statistical Breviary* (1801).

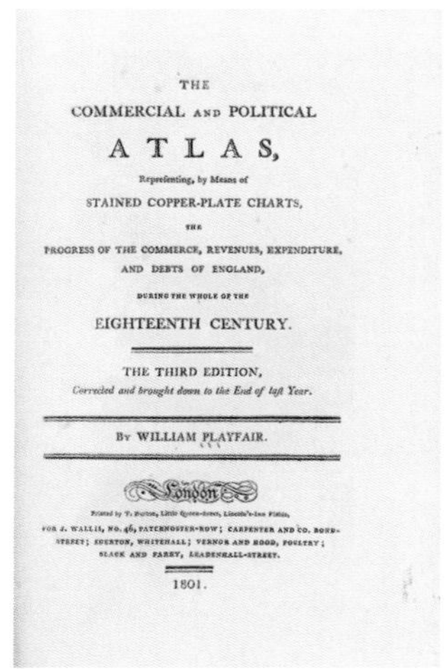

THE
COMMERCIAL AND POLITICAL
ATLAS,
Representing, by Means of
STAINED COPPER-PLATE CHARTS,
THE
PROGRESS OF THE COMMERCE, REVENUES, EXPENDITURE,
AND DEBTS OF ENGLAND,
DURING THE WHOLE OF THE
EIGHTEENTH CENTURY.

THE THIRD EDITION,
Corrected and brought down to the End of last Year.

BY WILLIAM PLAYFAIR.

London:
Printed by T. Burton, Little Queen-street, Lincoln's-Inn Fields,
FOR J. WALLIS, NO. 46, PATERNOSTER-ROW; CARPENTER AND CO. BOND-STREET; EGERTON, WHITEHALL; VERNOR AND HOOD, POULTRY; BLACK AND PARRY, LEADENHALL-STREET.

1801.

12

Figure 12 Front page of William Playfair, *The Commercial and Political Atlas,* 1786 (third edition, 1801)

Figure 13 Line charts: Exports & Imports to and from Denmark & Norway, Exports & Imports to and from Sweden. William Playfair, *The Commercial and Political Atlas,* 1786

Figure 14 This display more than two hundred years later uses William Playfair's three inventions: line, bar, and pie charts. *Transportvaneundersøgelsen, Faktaark om cykeltrafik i Danmark,* DTU Transport and the Danish National Travel Survey, 2013

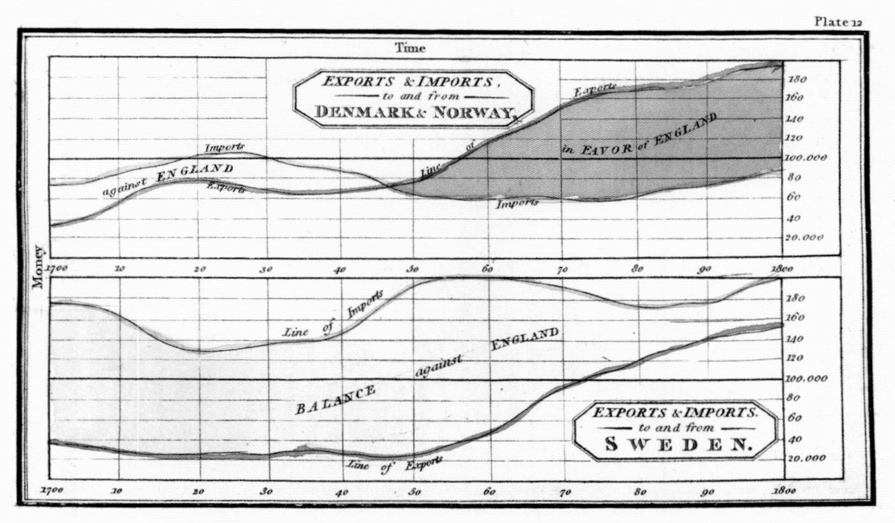

13

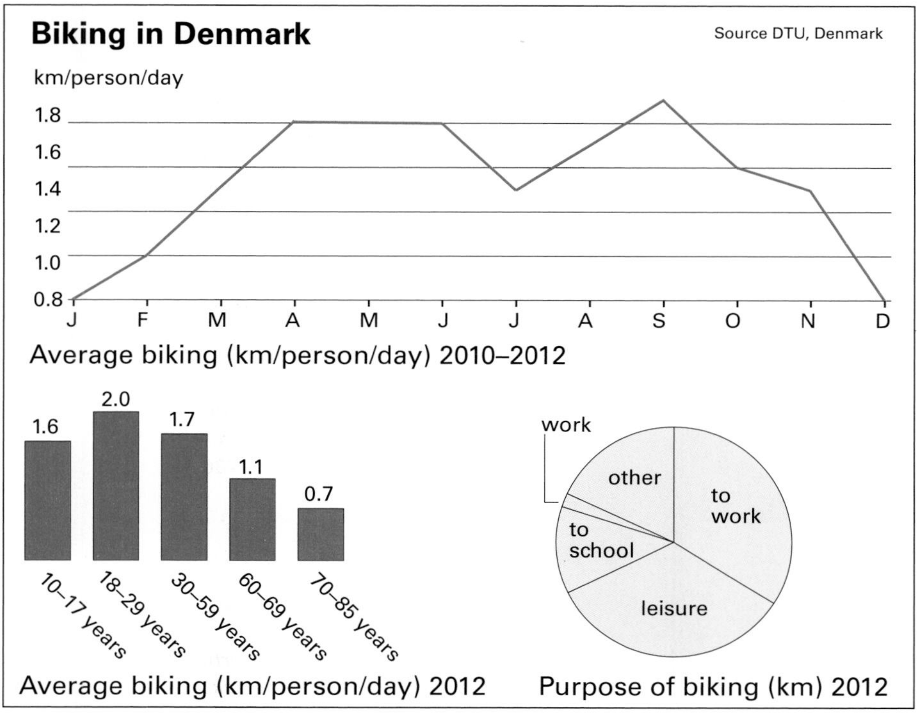

Biking in Denmark

Source DTU, Denmark

km/person/day

1.8
1.6
1.4
1.2
1.0
0.8

J F M A M J J A S O N D

Average biking (km/person/day) 2010–2012

1.6 2.0 1.7 1.1 0.7

10–17 years 18–29 years 30–59 years 60–69 years 70–85 years

Average biking (km/person/day) 2012

work
other
to work
to school
leisure

Purpose of biking (km) 2012

14

– *Taming quantities*

Otto Neurath (1882–1945), an Austrian sociologist, had didactics on his mind when he introduced his visual information displays. Neurath developed visual displays with pictorial symbols that were less abstract than Playfair's charts. Neurath and his team in Vienna developed Isotype – International System Of TYpographic Picture Education – an approach to data visualisation aimed at a broad audience. In picture tables pictograms replaced numbers, showing relevant economic and political quantities in ways that capture the attention.

Neurath developed Isotype – sometimes called the *Vienna Method of Pictorial Statistics* – to be used in the Gesellschafts- und Wirtschaftsmuseum in Wien, the Social and Economic Museum in Vienna, where he was founding director. The intended audience was ordinary visitors. Marie Reidemeister 'transformed' facts into graphics. German artist Gerd Arntz developed the graphic form.

Isotype was developed between 1925 and 1934 when the museum was closed for political reasons. The name *Isotype* was introduced in 1935 after Otto Neurath and Marie Reidemeister (from 1941, Marie Neurath) left Austria for the Netherlands. In 1942, they founded the Isotype Institute in England.

Figure 15 *Bildstatistik,* Picture statistics, vol 11, year 2, 1932/33. Gesellschafts- und Wirtschaftsmuseum in Wien. Otto and Marie Neurath Isotype Collection, University of Reading

BILDSTATISTIK

DES GESELLSCHAFTS- UND WIRTSCHAFTSMUSEUMS IN WIEN

JAHRGANG 2 • 1932/33 HEFT 11

Vereinigte Staaten von Nordamerika

Einwanderung in den Jahren 1821—1930

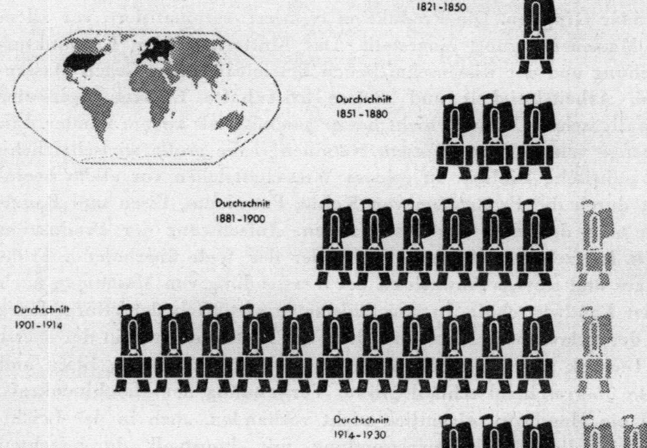

15

The size of pictograms in picture tables remains consistent throughout; they do not change size to show quantities. This principle built on Neurath's observation that it is easier and more precise to count a number of identical symbols than to compare pictorial symbols of different size. The picture tables were scaled: each symbol stood for one hundred, one thousand, one million, or another number of real-world units.

The great advantage of Isotype is that its repetitions of little men, cars, ships, etc. are entertaining; they capture and hold attention. Graphic designers value this advantage and occasionally use picture tables when naked figures without any graph would explain facts more easily and precisely.

Figure 16 Kraftwagenbestand der Erde, the automobiles of the world. *Gesellschaft und Wirtschaft, Society and economy,* Gesellschafts- und Wirtschaftsmuseum in Wien. Otto and Marie Neurath Isotype Collection, University of Reading

Figure 17 Arbeitslose, unemployment 1913–1928 in Great Britain, France, and Germany. *Gesellschaft und Wirtschaft, Society and economy,* Gesellschafts- und Wirtschaftsmuseum in Wien. Otto and Marie Neurath Isotype Collection, University of Reading

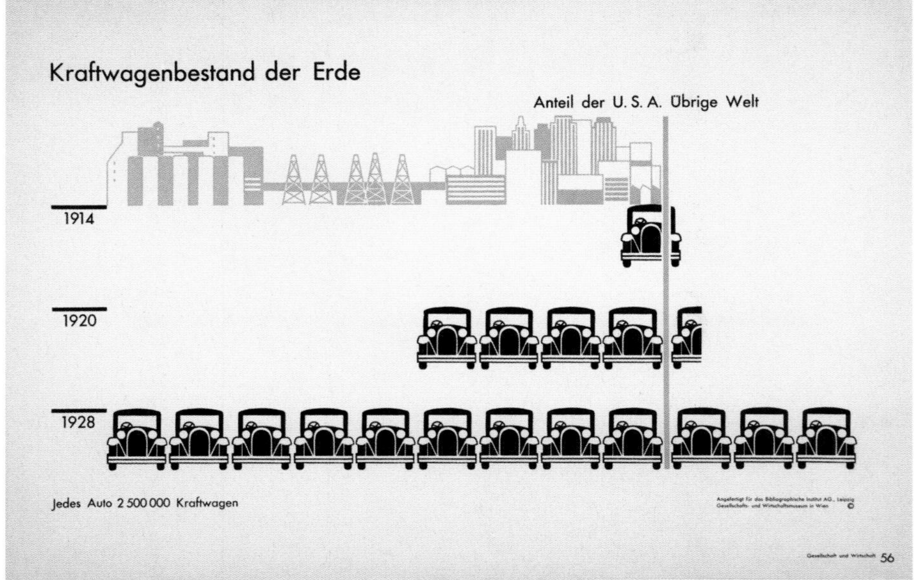

16

Arbeitslose
GROSSBRITANNIEN
FRANKREICH
DEUTSCHES REICH
1913
1920
1925
1926
1927
1928
Jede Figur 250 000 Arbeitslose
Angefertigt für das Bibliographische Institut AG., Leipzig
Gesellschafts- und Wirtschaftsmuseum in Wien ©
Gesellschaft und Wirtschaft 87

17

Beware of visual displays

Visual displays are everywhere today. We meet them every day in business reports, textbooks, newspapers, magazines, slide presentations, TV, and other digital media. Modern technology has made it easier to make and disseminate visual displays than in the past. But not all visual displays are good visual displays. Intentionally or not, they may be less than perfect.

– *Disinformation*

Political propagandists and real estate developers are occasionally tempted into using visual displays that bend the truth to benefit their own interests. Scales measuring growth can be distorted on line charts, while real estate maps can reduce or omit unappealing aspects. Visual displays can be used to disseminate misinformation as well as information.

– *Inaccuracy*

Apart from intentional lies, visual displays can hide the truth when designers lack professional skill. Typographic errors, incorrect data, wrong types of display, or sloppy displays can all misrepresent facts or hide the truth.

– *Lack of restraint*
Together with the ubiquity of visual displays we have also seen a certain lack of restraint. Some designers emphasise entertainment in place of clarity and representation; they design visual displays that are flashy and outlandish rather than factual and relevant. Comparing the size of a moon crater with a football field makes sense. Showing how far into space a stack of one-dollar bills would reach serves no purpose in explaining the US national debt.

– *Literature*
There is a growing number of books on data visualisation and visual displays. Some are uncritical in selecting practical examples, featuring colourful, but functionally poor, visual displays. These can be more confusing than informative, as it takes more time to understand how these displays work, and more time to read and understand the content than it would take to read and understand simple visual displays or naked numbers.

– *Simplicity again*
The great problem of contemporary data visualisation is not the lack of technical possibilities, but a lack of critical thinking by designers. Designers should master the basic principles rather than use unnecessarily complicated displays. Singers master basic singing techniques before performing demanding arias. Great singers know when simplicity serves the music best.

Research and common sense

Good visual displays should be based on sound research principles. In a time when design education at the world's leading design schools is undergoing a shift from a foundation in art, craft, and material to a foundation in research, the argument that visual displays should be research based appears logical. However, there are some howevers.

– *Designers don't have time*

For designers who often work to tight deadlines, research beyond use of well-understood practice is seldom an option. Experience and common sense are the guides.

– *Existing research results are often unavailable*

Few relevant research results are available to the graphic designer. *Graph Design for the Eye and Mind* by Stephen M. Kosslyn (2006) is one exception. It refers to scores of research results organised according to type of display.

Stephen M. Kosslyn
Graph Design for the Eye and Mind,
Oxford University Press,
New York, NY, 2006

– *Research results contradict each other*

Some of the results mentioned in Kosslyn's book contradict each other. Since readers don't know the specific circumstances of the research, it is difficult to have an informed opinion on what is right and what is wrong. We don't know the exact type of visual display considered, or details about audience, size, and qualifications.

– *Research results are obvious*
Research results which are not contradicted by other research results often appear self-evident to practising designers.

– *Lack of relevance*
The problem at hand is probably in one or more ways different from the problem on which the available research is based. However, designers with a robust foundation in research will know how to apply research from related but different problems.

– *User-based design*
If a research-based solution is not an option for one or more of the above reasons, then what about user-based design? A designer can make an early model of a proposed visual display for testing by relevant users. This permits response and discussion about the design principles that are used. User-based design is an option when time and finances permit.

If the complexity and importance of the project at hand are comparable to the design of a new map for a metro system, it is sensible to practise user-based design for ample user feedback at an early stage. This would prevent the kind of embarrassment that occurred when Transport for London launched a Tube map that did not show the River Thames. The map was soon withdrawn due to protests.

A 'furious' Boris Johnson [Mayor of London] has ordered the River Thames to be reinstated on the London Underground map after Transport for London decided to redesign it. TfL's decision to remove zone boundaries will also now be reviewed.
The government body today announced it would replace the maps after outcry from politicians and passenger groups – and fears that people could end up paying higher fares by accident.
Daily Mail, 18 Sep 2009

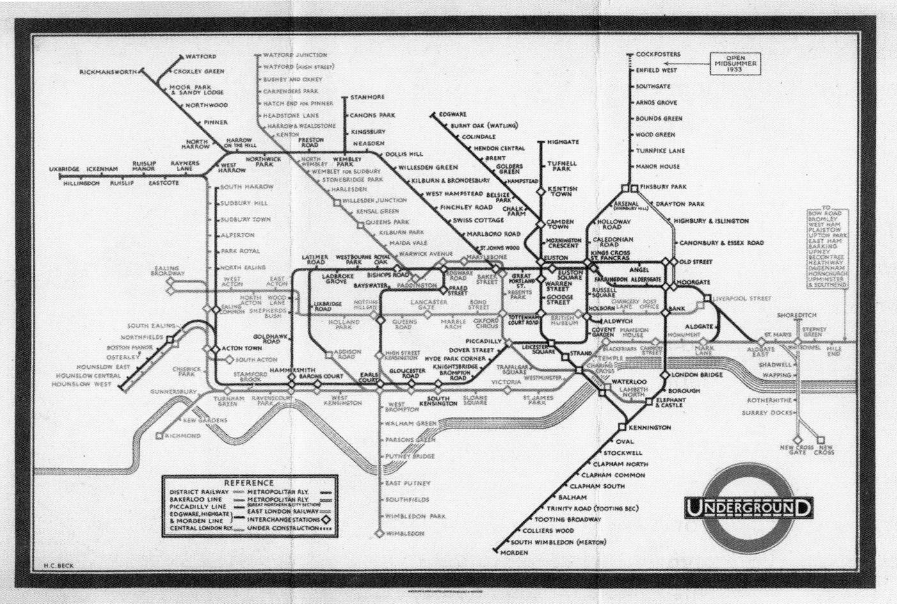

18

Figure 18 Henry C. Beck's Tube map from 1931 is the iconic map that all later transit map designers remember, admire, and refer to. Beck knew that it was not enough to show the stations and the lines. The river Thames was the supporting element that allowed passengers to relate the system to the terrain. In his description* of the genesis of the map Beck did not mention the inclusion of the only surface feature on the map. He must have taken its presence for granted. Courtesy of the London Transport Museum

*Written for Ken Garland and referred to in:
Garland, Ken
Mr. Beck's Underground Map
Capital Transport Publishing, Harrow Weald, 1994

However, visual display designers will typically work in situations where neither research nor user-based design is possible because time and finances don't allow it. Designers must rely on heuristics, rules of thumb based on well-published research results, professional experience, and common sense – which, according to Voltaire, was not so common. In doing so, the experienced designer will remember that in practical life as in science, truth is only truth until new knowledge emerges.

Gestalt principles of perception

The Law of Prägnanz (German for pithiness) says that our minds tend to refine what we actually see to create order in our impression and understanding of a cluttered world. Gestalt principles describe some of the ways our minds organise what we actually see. The designer of visual displays can use gestalt principles in two ways: to create effective solutions, and to check a design for possible unwanted reactions. How will the reader see this display?

Laws of
- closure
- similarity
- proximity
- symmetry
- continuity
- common fate

– *The law of closure*

We tend to replace what seems to be missing. The law of closure describes how we connect separate visual fragments to create a visual whole. This happens particularly in the case of simple, easily recognisable, geometric patterns, e.g. circles. We tend to see a circle formed by unconnected elements before we see the individual elements separately. The reader completes fragments to create a visual whole. In visual displays this is probably of less importance than in logo design.

19

Figure 19 Walker with missing legs. The law of closure: we see Johnnie Walker of the eponymous whisky even though the walking legs are missing; our mind fills in the blanks. Courtesy of Diageo

– *The law of similarity*
We tend to group similar objects together to see them as a family. This is what happens when we watch sports games where competing teams are dressed in different colours. In visual displays the principle can be used both to group and diversify different kinds of information. The principle points to an economy of means: changes in form should be used only to communicate changes in content.

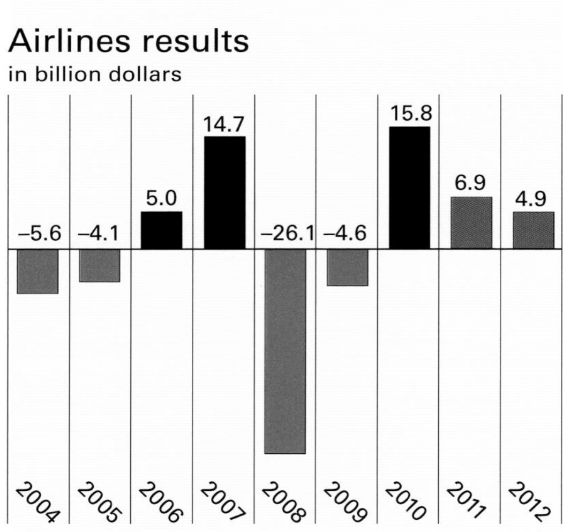

20

Figure 20 The vertical bar chart shows the financial results of international airlines. In printed accounts, negative profits are traditionally printed with red figures. When showing financial results on a bar chart, it is a good idea to keep this colour coding; the law of similarity at play.
It is also a good idea to make a colour distinction between realised and expected results.
Data sourced from *Frankfurter Allgemeine Zeitung*, DE, 21 Sep 2011

– *The law of proximity*
We perceive things located near each other as belonging together, and things located far from each other as separate. In cars, we expect to find all the instruments and buttons for the radio next to one another. In visual displays, this principle says that labels should be placed closer to the entity they identify and describe than to any other.

See note on the design of *Data Design, p8*

– *The law of symmetry*
Symmetry is about recognisable repetition. In visual displays, the same type of elements can be used in the same ways to enable easy reading. Readers recognise and recall certain types of information better if they are treated in similar ways.

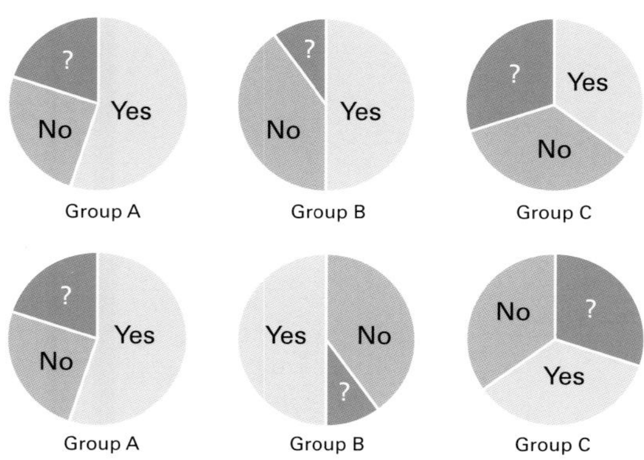

Figure 21 According to the law of symmetry, it is easier to compare three pie charts if the parts are organised in identical order (top) rather than different order (bottom).

– The law of continuity

We tend to see elements that are aligned as belonging together in one whole. In designing visual displays, the law of continuity tells us to align graphic elements with purpose and care.

– The law of common fate

We perceive objects that move in the same direction as belonging together. As far as visual displays are concerned, the law of common fate is relevant in dynamic displays in digital media. The law tells us to move information that belongs together at the same time and in the same direction, and to avoid movements not doing so.

Figure 22 Ballots from the 2000 presidential elections in Florida.
Ballots not respecting the law of continuity (bad alignment) resulted in many voters being confused and consequently giving their vote to an unwanted candidate. By mistake, they voted for Pat Buchanan instead of Al Gore and thereby helped George W. Bush to win.

22

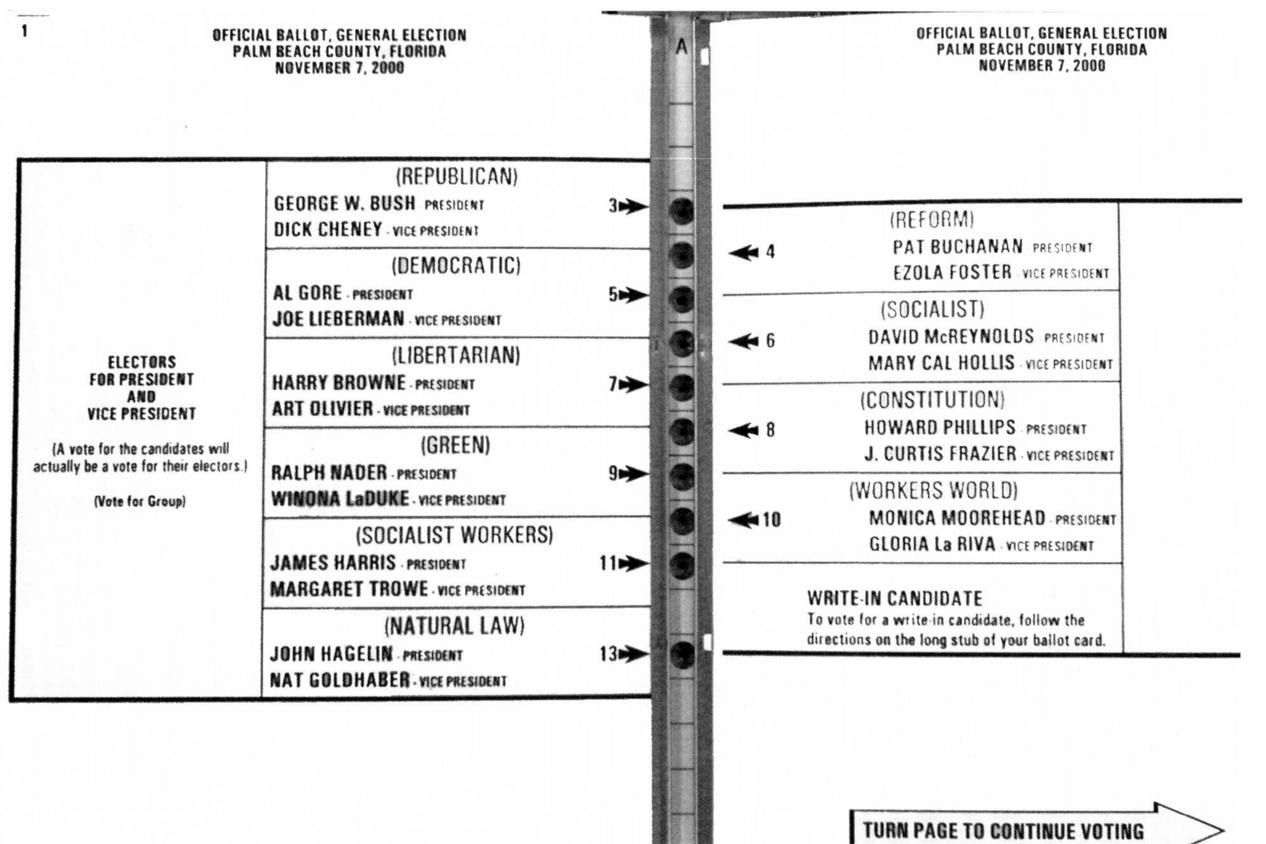
1

OFFICIAL BALLOT, GENERAL ELECTION
PALM BEACH COUNTY, FLORIDA
NOVEMBER 7, 2000

ELECTORS
FOR PRESIDENT
AND
VICE PRESIDENT

(A vote for the candidates will actually be a vote for their electors.)

(Vote for Group)

(REPUBLICAN)
GEORGE W. BUSH PRESIDENT
DICK CHENEY · VICE PRESIDENT
3 ➜

(DEMOCRATIC)
AL GORE · PRESIDENT
JOE LIEBERMAN · VICE PRESIDENT
5 ➜

(LIBERTARIAN)
HARRY BROWNE · PRESIDENT
ART OLIVIER · VICE PRESIDENT
7 ➜

(GREEN)
RALPH NADER · PRESIDENT
WINONA LaDUKE · VICE PRESIDENT
9 ➜

(SOCIALIST WORKERS)
JAMES HARRIS · PRESIDENT
MARGARET TROWE · VICE PRESIDENT
11 ➜

(NATURAL LAW)
JOHN HAGELIN · PRESIDENT
NAT GOLDHABER · VICE PRESIDENT
13 ➜

A

OFFICIAL BALLOT, GENERAL ELECTION
PALM BEACH COUNTY, FLORIDA
NOVEMBER 7, 2000

(REFORM)
◀ 4
PAT BUCHANAN PRESIDENT
EZOLA FOSTER · VICE PRESIDENT

(SOCIALIST)
◀ 6
DAVID McREYNOLDS PRESIDENT
MARY CAL HOLLIS · VICE PRESIDENT

(CONSTITUTION)
◀ 8
HOWARD PHILLIPS · PRESIDENT
J. CURTIS FRAZIER · VICE PRESIDENT

(WORKERS WORLD)
◀ 10
MONICA MOOREHEAD · PRESIDENT
GLORIA La RIVA · VICE PRESIDENT

WRITE-IN CANDIDATE
To vote for a write-in candidate, follow the directions on the long stub of your ballot card.

TURN PAGE TO CONTINUE VOTING

Psychological principles

Stephen M. Kosslyn describes eight psychological principles that lie behind the way we perceive and comprehend visual displays. Kosslyn calls all visual displays *graphs*. Designers should know the eight principles and use them to establish and check the functionality of their visual displays. Kosslyn's eight principles are summarised below.

Stephen M. Kosslyn
Graph Design for the Eye and Mind,
Oxford University Press, New York, NY, 2006

– *The principle of relevance*
Keep the purpose of the visual display in mind. Don't confuse readers with irrelevant details.

– *The principle of appropriate knowledge*
Know the audience and address it appropriately. Don't talk down to intended readers, or talk over their heads. Use language and concepts intended readers are likely to know.

– *The principle of salience*
Make new parts of the display more visible than old, already-known parts. In a geographic map showing a proposed coast-to-coast railway across North America, the outline of North America is the old part, while the suggested railway line is the new part.

– *The principle of perceptual organisation*
Perhaps the least operational of Kosslyn's eight principles, this deals with the ways our mind organises and interprets what we see. Sometimes we see two-dimensional phenomena as three-dimensional, sometimes we fail to isolate one visual effect but combine it with others, and sometimes we group elements in ways that influence our impression. The best advice concerning the principle of perceptual organisation is to test visual displays for usability.

– *The principle of discriminability*
When parts must be distinguished, make the visual difference between these parts as clear as possible.

– *The principle of compatibility*
Let visual displays represent the facts of the world in a logical way. Represent high prices by high curves. Show left-wing politics on the left side of a visual display and right-wing politics on the right.

– *The principle of informative changes*
Show differences in meaning by difference in form. Restrict changes in form to show changes in meaning.

– *The principle of capacity limitations*
Readers are only human. Keep the limits of readers' perceptive and cognitive capacities in mind when designing visual displays. Know the readers and don't overload them.

Colour

Colour is used to represent all three subjects of *Data Design*: quantities, locations, and connections. Colours can be described in several ways, but here we shall describe colours as we see them. They include three elements: hue, value, and saturation.

– *Hue*
Hue is what most people normally understand as colour. All hues are found on the colour circle, also called *the colour wheel.*

– *Value*
The value of a colour concerns its blackness or whiteness. It stands for the amount of black or white added to the hue found on the colour circle.

– *Saturation*
The saturation of a colour is defined as its absence of white and black. The maximum saturated hues are found on the colour circle. The more we move away from the colour circle to approach grey, the less saturated the colour is.

– *NCS*
The NCS Natural Colour System®©
describes how the three colour dimensions play together.

The NCS facilitates understanding of the colour properties. For working specifications, designers use CMYK for print, RGB for screens, and hexadecimal values specifically for web design.

Figure 23 The NCS Colour Space. A double cone, where all maximum saturated hues constituting the colour circle are found on the 'equator' and black and white are found on opposite poles.
Courtesy of NCS

Figure 24 The NCS Colour Circle. A horizontal section through the 'equator' of the NCS Colour Space gives a circle with all hues on its periphery.
Courtesy of NCS

Figure 25 The NCS Colour Triangle. A vertical section from the surface towards the centre of the NCS Colour Space gives a triangle with a maximum saturated hue at one point ('equator') and black and white on the two remaining points (poles).
A straight line through the cone from pole to pole is a pure greyscale.
Courtesy of NCS

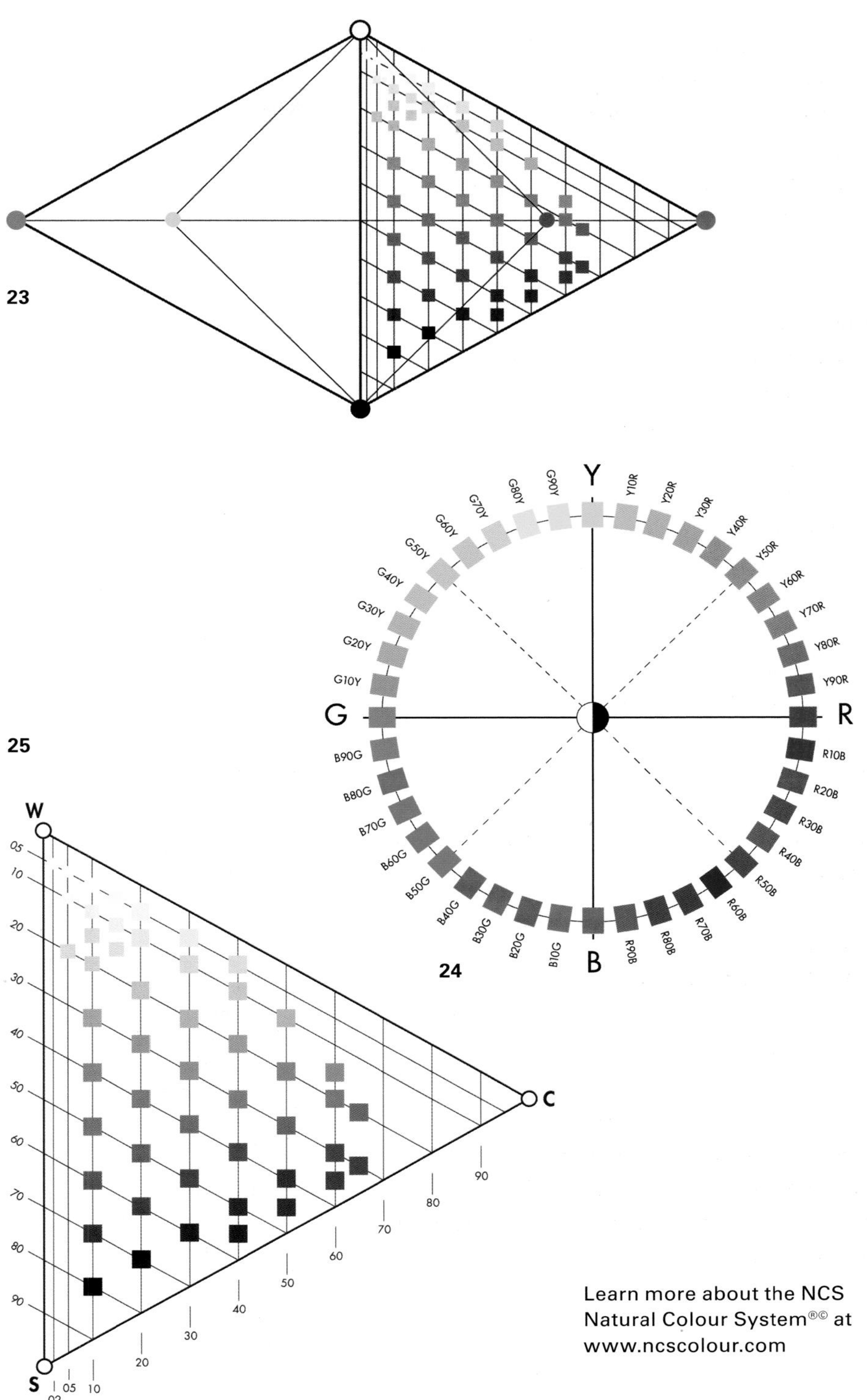

Learn more about the NCS Natural Colour System®© at www.ncscolour.com

– *Use of colour*

The first role of colour in visual displays is to differentiate and convey meaning. The second role is to make the displays attractive. To fulfil the first role, colour must change to represent changes in meaning, and only then.

The kind of change in colour should reflect the kind of change in meaning. Semantic colour use can sometimes build on standard colour conventions. For example, bars in bar charts can change from black to red, when financial results become negative. Other uses of colour in displays may be culturally conditioned.

Semantic colour use can also build on analogy: one element represented with outstanding colour is also outstanding in importance. Similar, but not identical, colours stand for similar, but not identical, entities.

As a general rule, colour should be used with restraint in visual displays. Too much colour emphasises nothing. It is a good idea to work with a limited palette, a small selection of systematically chosen colours, and stick to them throughout a project.

Figure 26 Greyscales with ten, five, and three steps.

Figure 27 Single hue progression from low to maximum saturation with ten, five, and three steps.

Figure 28 Bipolar hot/cold progression with seven steps.

Figure 29 Bipolar bad/ good progression with seven steps. *See Dorling cartograms p135.*

Figure 30 Spectral colour range with six steps.

26

27

28

29

30

Notation

Complete visual displays require a text to explain the theme of the display and, perhaps, how it works.

– *Title*
The title of a visual display can be at the top of the display or at the bottom. There are two ways of titling a visual display: neutral and interpretative: the situation determines which to use. If both are used, the neutral title should come first, and the interpretative title second.

– *Neutral title*
One way of titling a visual display is to identify what the display is about in neutral terms. For example 'German car export 2000–2010'. This method requires the reader to find out what is significant in the display.

– *Interpretative title*
The other way of titling a visual display is to announce the message of the display. For example 'German car exports rise drastically'. This method is more journalistic: it takes the reader by the hand. Some may argue that this type of titling is redundant.

– *Labels*
Labels identify and explain the elements of the visual display. Direct labels are placed inside or adjacent to the elements they describe. A pointer, a thin line from label to element, may assist adjacent labels.

Figure 31 Visual display complete with neutral title, labels along the axes, and a legend. A caption could have explained why the production peeked in 1992/93. An extra legend could have explained that a metric ton of oil equals something around seven barrels (depends on the density of the oil).
Image is in the public domain

– *Legend*

A legend – or key – is an indirect label that describes the code of visual variables without direct labels. It is most often placed in the lower right corner of the display.

– *Captions*

Captions draw attention to and explain issues of special interest.

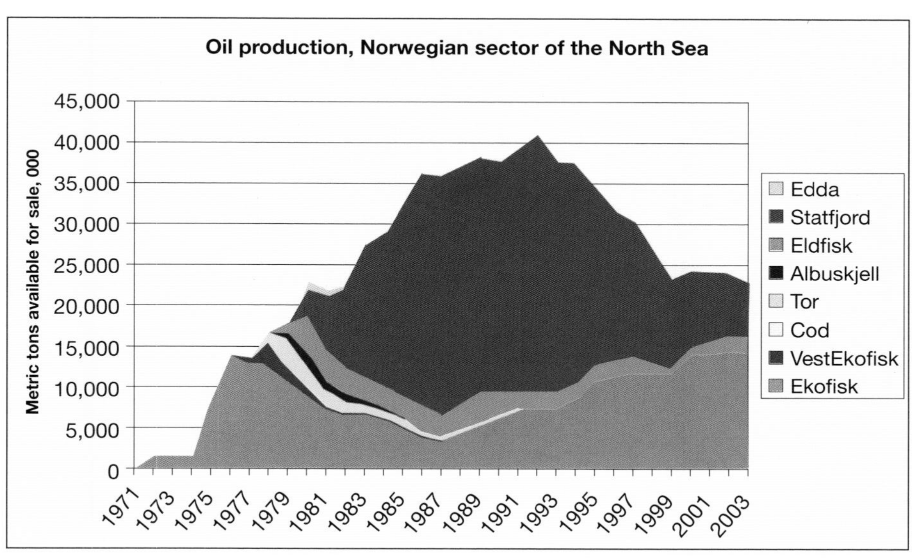

31

Reading visual displays

In *Semiology of Graphics* (1983), Jacques Bertin describes three levels of reading visual displays: elementary, intermediate, and overall reading. Bertin refers to visual displays as *graphics*.

Jacques Bertin
Semiology of Graphics,
University of Wisconsin
Press, Madison, WI, 1983

The designer of visual displays should have these three levels of reading in mind. Some displays must enable reading on all three levels; some only need to be read on one or two levels.

– *Elementary reading*
Elementary reading implies looking at a single relationship between variables, for instance in a time series showing Norwegian oil production 1971–2003 to determine when production peaked *(see figure 31).*

– *Intermediate reading*
Intermediate reading implies looking at a part of a visual display greater than the single relationship but smaller than the totality, for example the development of Norwegian oil production after the year 2000 *(see figure 31).*

– *Overall reading*
Overall reading implies looking at the totality of the visual display, for example the trend of the Norwegian oil production 1971–2003 *(see figure 31).*

Basics

Choice of display

Every design of a visual display ideally starts by defining its purpose and use. We must ask 'Why do we want this display?' Different types of visual displays have different capacities for answering different questions. The correct choice of display is important. The following questions help to determine the right visual display:

The generic question to be answered will head each display presentation in *Data Design.*

- What kind of questions must the visual display answer?

- What kind of data is available?

- What kind of reading should be enabled: elementary, intermediate, overall?

- What kind of readers will the display address? What are their capacities for understanding visual displays and special concepts and terms?

- What media must be used: print or computer for careful reading, or TV or smartphone for fast reading?

- Which types of display are appropriate to this visualisation? Which is the best?

The designer of visual displays should always ask how the intended visual display is superior to a pure verbal and numerical explanation and in what ways this is so. Visual displays that don't offer improved reading in terms of perception and cognition should perhaps not be designed.

Visualising quantities

How much? This is the question most often addressed by visual displays. Quantities are interesting, and visual displays tell the story in understandable, fact-revealing, attention-getting, and memorable ways.

The development of standard displays such as line, bar, and pie charts has contributed to the popularity of quantitative displays. After more than two hundred years in use, these displays are still the most frequently seen.

Before the presentation of several types of visual displays, a chapter on variables discusses the nature of data variation. Understanding the basic concepts of data variation is essential when discussing the various types of display.

"The advantage proposed by this method is not that of giving a more accurate statement than by figures, but it is to give a more simple and permanent idea of the gradual progress and comparative amounts, at different periods, by presenting to the eye a figure, the proportions of which correspond with the amounts of the sums intended to be expressed." William Playfair, *The Commercial and Political Atlas*, 1786, *ppIX–X*

Variables

A variable is a factor that may vary. In a line chart showing the amount of crime in a certain number of years, the amount of crime and the time are variables.

A quantitative relationship represented by a visual display can have one or more independent variables and one or more dependent variables.

– *Independent variables*
An independent variable describes the circumstance or the subject of a measurement. In the example of crime in X-ville *(figure 32)*, time is an independent variable. The years constitute the circumstance under which the amount of crime is measured. In a bar chart that compares sales in three departments *(figure 33)*, department is the independent variable. It constitutes the subject.

– *Dependent variables*
A dependent variable is a variable that may change when the value of an independent variable changes. In the examples given here, the amount of crime and the sales in the departments are dependent variables. They may change over time or with respect to one department or another.

In medical research, the treatment is the independent variable while the effect on the patient is the dependent variable. The independent variable is manipulated, and its effect upon the patient is measured.

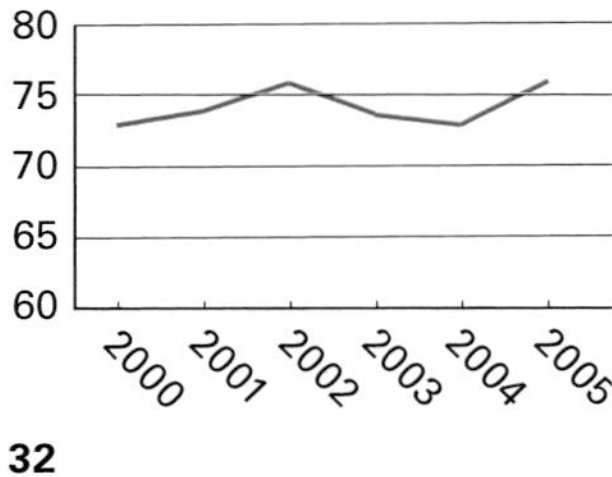

32

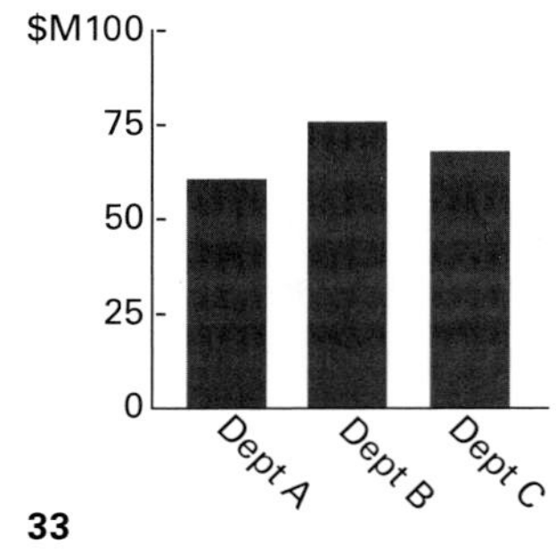

33

Figure 32 Line chart.

Figure 33 Vertical bar chart.

Variables are classified according to their organisation: categorical, ordered, and quantitative.

– Categorical variation

Categorical variables are known by their distinctive difference, by their lack of universal order, and by not being quantifiable. Gender is a categorical variable. Breed of dogs is also a categorical variable, and so is blood type. There is no order or quantitative relation between the sexes, between the breeds of dogs, or between blood types.

Categorical variation is also called *nominal* or *qualitative variation.*

– Ordered variation

Ordered variables are like categorical variables apart from one thing: they have a universal order. Encounters specified as a first, second, and third kind involve an ordered variable. That the three values have numbers doesn't make them quantitative. The numbers are ordinal; they indicate order, not quantity. Academic degree specified as bachelor's, master's, and doctorate is another example of an ordered variable. It is organised by a universal order.

Ordered variation is also called *ordinal variation.*

– Quantitative variation

Quantitative variables are known and distinguished by values that can be counted or measured and stated in cardinal numbers. The amount of crime in different cities and the sales in different departments are examples of quantitative variables. Quantitative variables also have all the properties of categorical and ordered variables.

Quantitative variation is also called *numerical variation.*

Quantitative variables are sometimes divided into interval variables and ratio variables.

Interval variables have fixed intervals and no natural zero. Interval variables also have all the properties of ordered and categorical variables.

Ratio variables have all the properties of interval, ordered, and categorical variables plus a natural zero where nothing exists. Temperature measured by the Kelvin scale is a ratio variable because the scale has a natural zero. On the other hand, temperature measured by the Fahrenheit, Celsius, or Reaumur scale is an interval variable as these scales do not have a natural zero.

The point of time when something happens is an interval variable; there is no zero point of time. The length of time something takes is a ratio variable; zero length of time does exist.

The distinction between interval and ratio variables plays no role for the displays discussed in *Data Design*. Categorical, ordered, and quantitative variables are the relevant categories in the visual displays shown.

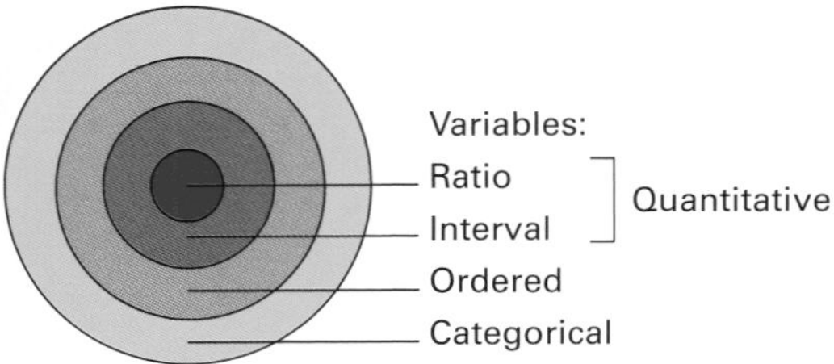

A variable is measured in relation to a scale, that represents the possible values the variable can have. Categorical variables are measured on categorical scales, ordered variables on ordered scales, and quantitative variables on quantitative scales.

Variables can be discrete or continuous.

Categorical and ordered variables are discrete.

Quantitative variables can be either discrete or continuous.

– *Discrete variables*
Discrete variables can only have certain values. The count of a woman's pregnancies is a discrete variable. It can only be a whole number.

– *Continuous variables*
Continuous variables can have any value, sometimes within a certain range. The height of sequoia trees can have any value within a certain range, so can a person's weight.

The average number of children per class in a school is a continuous variable. It can have any value specified with however many decimals. The number of children in one specific school class, however, is a discrete variable. It can only be a whole number.

Pie charts

How do parts of a whole compare with each other and with the whole?

Pie charts are also known as *circle charts*.

Pie charts divide a whole into parts that stand for percentages or fractions and enable comparison of the parts and the whole. The sum of the parts, the full pie, represents a whole, 100 per cent. The parts of the pie are called *slices* or *wedges*.

Other chart types that compare parts of a whole include:
- Donut charts, *p66*
- Divided-bar charts, *p82*
- Treemaps, *p149*

The independent variable in a pie chart – what is measured – is categorical. It is represented by the slices. The dependent variable – the measurement – is quantitative. It is represented by the size of the slices. In a pie chart that shows how a market is shared by four companies, company is the independent variable, while market share is the dependent variable.

To enable fast reading and comparison the slices of a pie chart must be identified with labels, preferably within the slices, or, if this is not possible, adjacent to them.

Pie charts capture and hold attention, but do not always give faster, and never more precise, information than raw percentages without a pie chart. If exact information about the percentages of the single slices is needed, percentage values should be given within, or adjacent to, the respective slices.

Figure 34 Use white or black division lines between the slices dependent on the darkness of the slices.

Figure 35 Pie chart with direct labels, three on and one adjacent to the relevant slices.

Figure 36 Direct labels (A) are preferable to a legend (B).

Figure 37 Strictly speaking this pie chart (A) is a hybrid between a display and a table. If exact percentages or absolute numbers are needed, it is always worth considering whether stating the raw percentages (B) would be preferable to the pie chart.

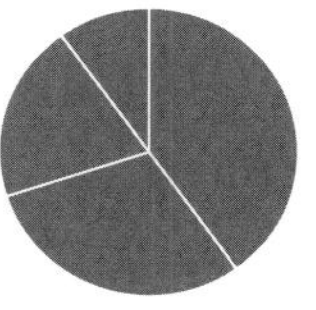

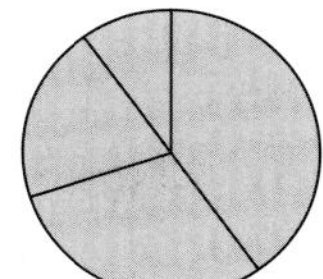

34

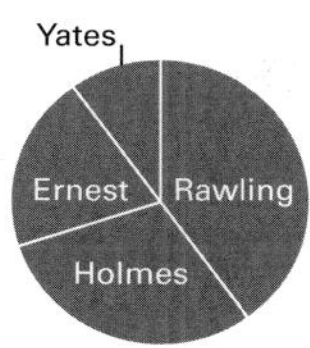

35

Cannabis referendum?
Do we need a referendum
on legalising cannabis?

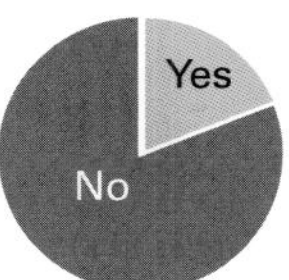

36A

Cannabis referendum?
Do we need a referendum
on legalising cannabis?

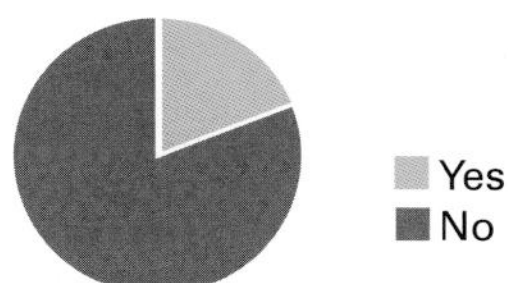

36B

Cannabis referendum?
Do we need a referendum
on legalising cannabis?

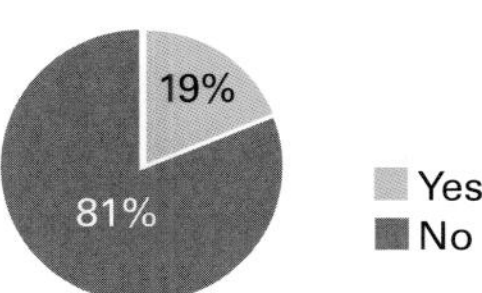

37A

Cannabis referendum?
Do we need a referendum
on legalising cannabis?

YES 19%
NO 81%

37B

Giving a pie chart an outlandish shape or making it three-dimensional can hinder fast reading and precise understanding.

If several pie charts are used side by side for comparison, slices representing similar entities, e.g. 'Yes', 'No', and 'Don't know', should be shown in the same order and, if applicable, be given the same hues or greytones. Hues and greytones can be explained in a legend to avoid repetition.

Pie charts can always be substituted by divided-bar charts (*see p82*). Divided-bar charts are less eye-catching than pie charts, but they can also show accumulated percentages. When divisions of several wholes must be compared, divided-bar charts give the fastest, and most precise, reading.

Figure 38 Organise slices with the largest slice at 12 o'clock and continue in falling order (A). One exception to this rule is that a category 'Other' should always be the last slice (B). Pie charts with three slices 'Yes', 'No', and 'Don't know' should be organised in that order (C).

Figure 39 If colour is wanted for conspicuousness in a pie chart, the slices can be given shades of grey or a hue, or different hues.

Figure 40 One slice can be emphasised, with a brighter or darker shade (A, B), or hue (C), or with explosion (D). Don't emphasise more than one slice and don't explode a slice larger than 40%.

Figure 41 Pie charts with very little information can sometimes be used rhetorically.

Figure 42 If a part of a pie chart must be broken into parts, it should be done in a bar chart, vertical or horizontal, not in a new pie chart.

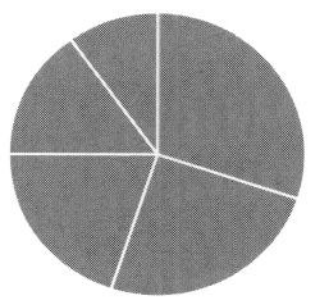

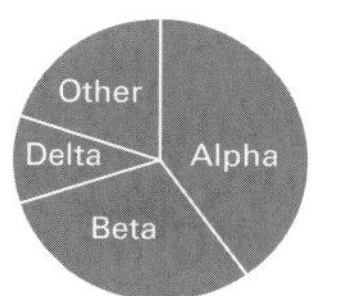

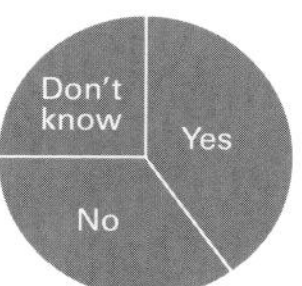

38A **38B** **38C**

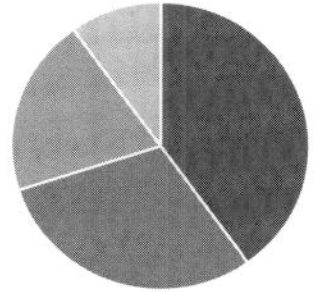

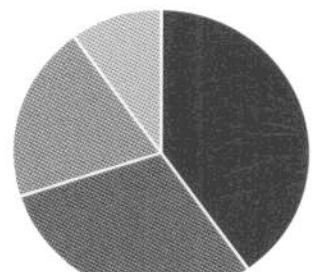

39

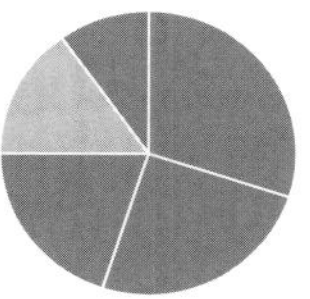

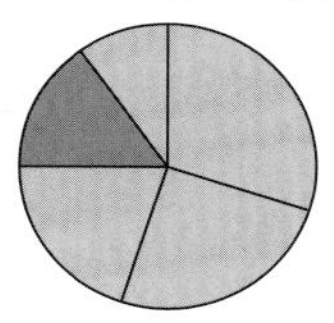

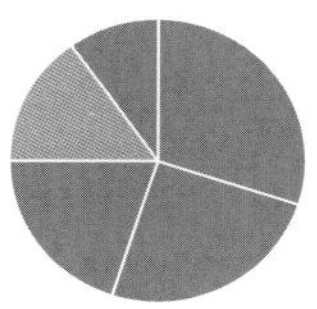

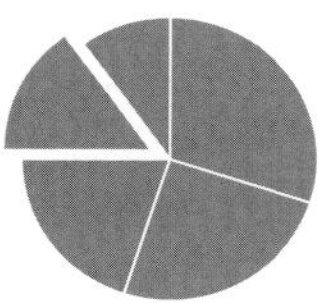

40A **40B** **40C** **40D**

Something then and now

Year 1980

37%

Today

29%

41

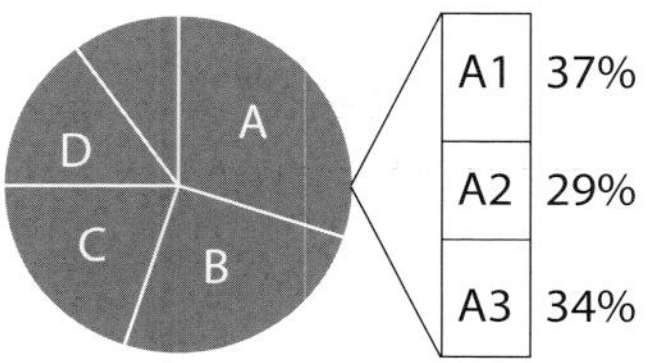

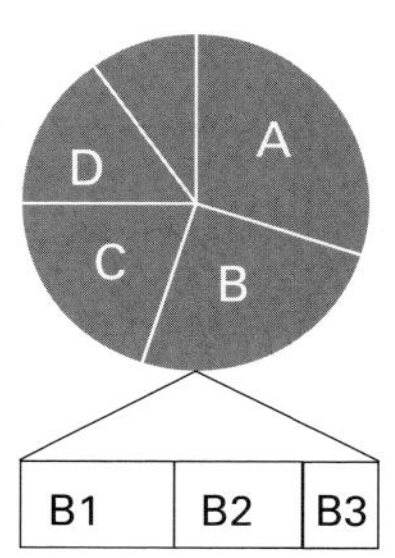

42

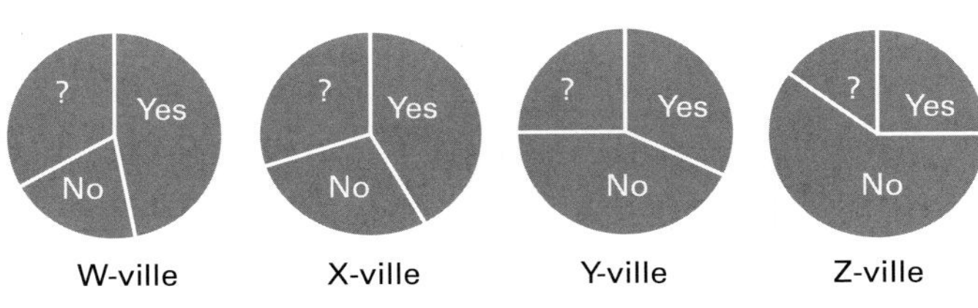

43

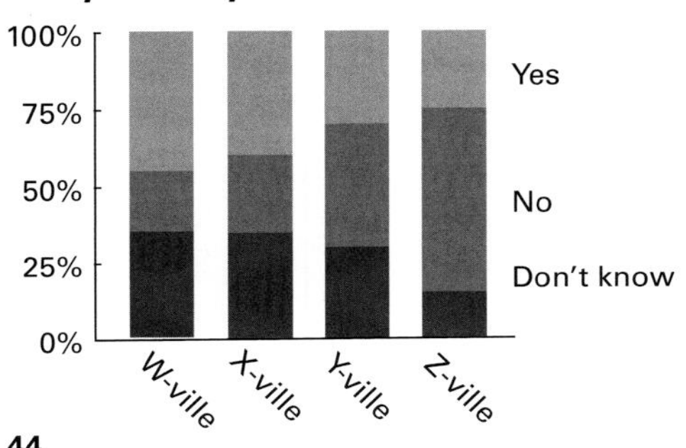

44

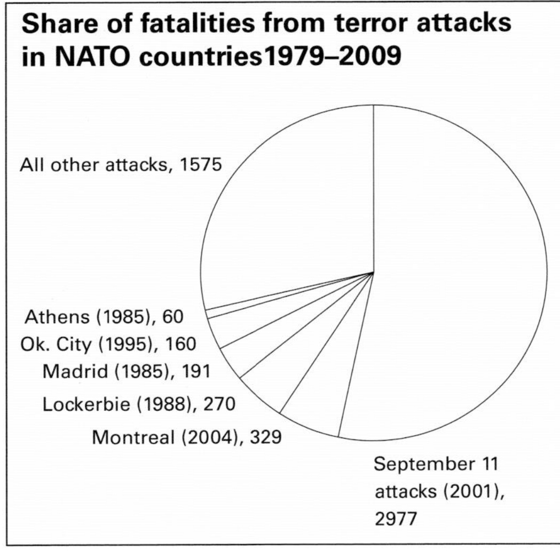

45

Figure 43 It may be problematic to compare several pie charts side by side. Sometimes divided-bar charts should be considered.

Figure 44 Divided-bar chart presenting the same information as given by the pie charts in figure 43.

Figure 45 Occasionally pie charts work fine with more than five slices.
Data and design concept sourced from Nate Silver *The Signal and the Noise, 2012, p439*

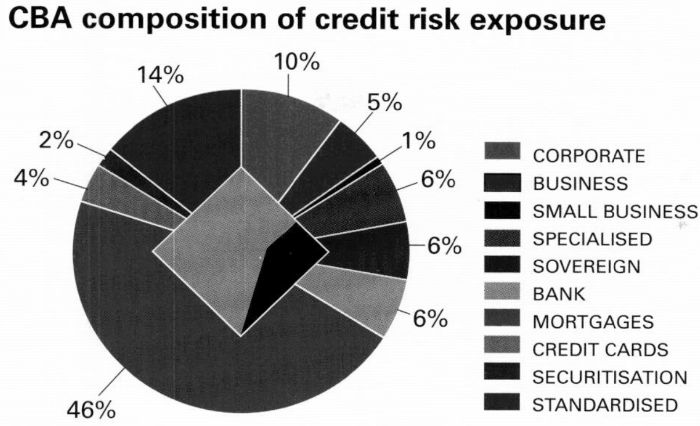

46

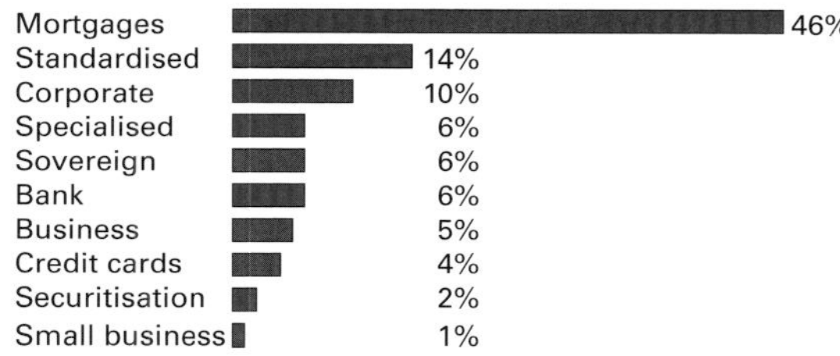

47

DON'T DO THIS

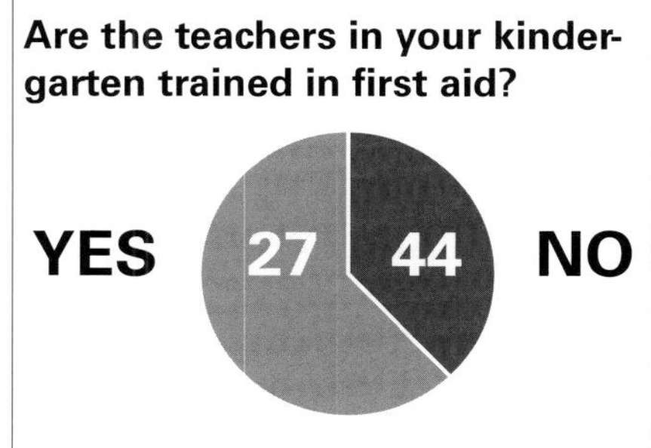

48

Figure 46 Pie charts with more than five or six slices can be problematic. Instead of a pie with ten slices, a horizontal bar chart could have been used to show the Commonwealth Bank's credit risk exposures. Data and design concept sourced from *The Australian*, AU, 16 Nov 2011

Figure 47 A horizontal bar chart showing the same data as (figure 46). Apart from giving a faster read, the horizontal bar chart also shows rank.

Figure 48 Don't use absolute numbers in pie charts. Readers expect to see percentages and become confused.

Donut charts

How do parts of a whole compare with each other and with the whole?

Donut charts are also known as *bagel charts*.

Donut charts are pie charts with a hole in the middle. Like pie charts, donut charts divide a whole into parts and enable comparison of the parts and the whole. The sum of the parts, the full pie, represents 100 per cent. The parts are called *segments*. The independent variable of a donut chart, represented by the segments, is categorical. The dependent variable, represented by the size of the segments, is quantitative. In a donut chart that shows how four landowners share an area, landowner is the independent variable, while land share is the dependent variable.

Other chart types that compare parts of a whole include:
- Pie charts, *p60*
- Divided-bar charts, *p82*
- Treemaps, *p149*

The hole in the middle of the donut chart is sometimes used for some information, typically the absolute total value of the content.

The decisive advantage of donut charts is their conspicuousness. They attract attention.

In terms of giving fast and precise information, donut charts are inferior to pie charts. When we 'read' a pie chart, we compare areas, angles, and arcs. In a donut chart the arcs remain unchanged, the areas become drastically smaller, and the angles practically disappear.

Figure 49 Donut charts can be extremely conspicuous. News editors like this feature.

Figure 50 Sometimes the hole in a donut chart is used to state the absolute amount.

Figure 51 To understand this donut, you must first read the legend. Once the legend is read, there is no reason to consult the donut.
Data and design concept sourced from *Monocle*, Issue 12, 2008

Figure 52 A pie chart with the smallest slices gathered in 'Nations with shares smaller than 5%' gives the essential information of figure 51 faster.

Landowners in Oakley Park

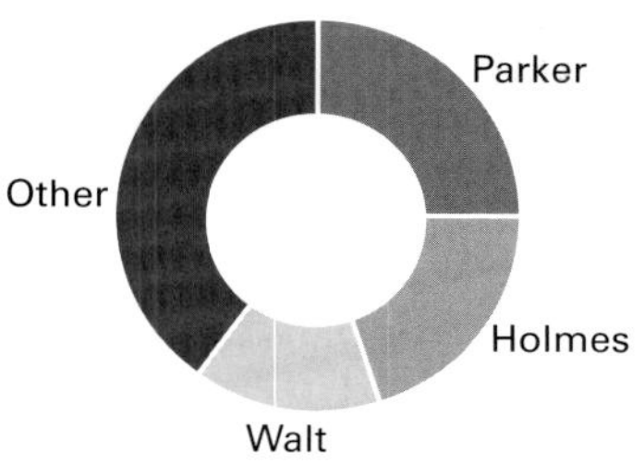

49

Landowners in Oakley Park

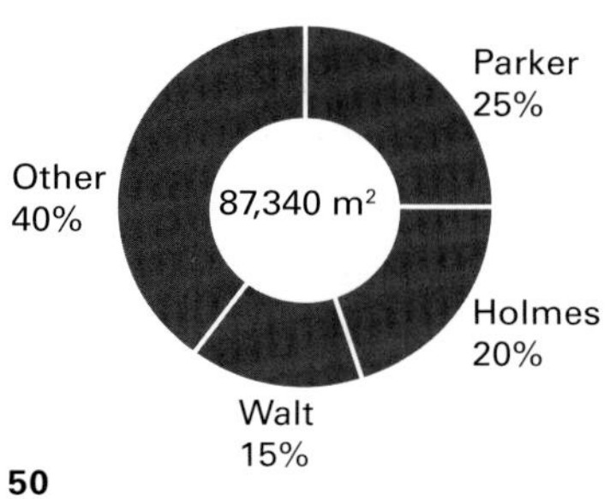

50

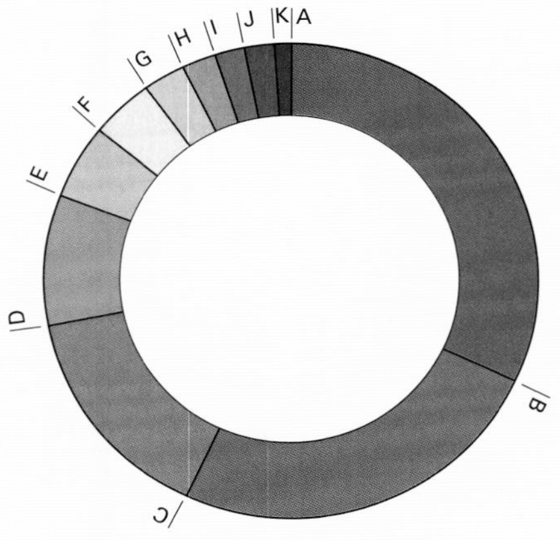

Foreign students in Australian higher education

A	Other	46,048	32%
B	China	37,803	25%
C	India	22,154	15%
D	Malaysia	14,359	9%
E	Hong Kong	7,699	5%
F	Indonesia	6,756	4%
G	Republic of Korea	5,078	3%
H	Thailand	3,786	2%
I	Japan	2,697	2%
J	USA	2,455	2%
K	Brazil	422	1%
	Total 149,257		

51

Foreign students in Australian higher education

Nations with shares smaller than 5%
46%
25%
China
15%
India
5
9%
Malaysia
Hong Kong

China	37,803	25%
India	22,154	15%
Malaysia	14,359	9%
Hong Kong	7,699	5%
Indonesia	6,756	4%
Republic of Korea	5,078	3%
Thailand	3,786	2%
Japan	2,697	2%
USA	2,455	2%
Brazil	422	1%
Other	46,048	32%
Total	149,257	100%

52

Vertical bar charts

How do items compare in absolute amounts?
How do items rank?

Vertical bar charts compare a limited number of relationships between an independent and a dependent variable.

The independent variable shown along the x axis can be categorical or ordered. The dependent variable shown along the y axis is quantitative.

The baseline in bar charts should always be at zero. Otherwise we wouldn't be able to compare the bars and see the true relationships *(see figure 53)*.

In vertical bar charts only the height, not the width, of the bars signifies value. However, the width should be large enough to capture attention. All bars should have the same width. The horizontal distance between the bars can be 50 per cent of the bar width.

If the independent variable is categorical, the bars, for example representing competing teams, can be reordered to show increasing or decreasing rank of athletes, research departments, etc.

Don't make vertical bar charts three-dimensional. They are more difficult to read.

Vertical bar charts are also known as *column charts*.

Other chart types that compare absolute amounts include:
- Horizontal bar charts, *p78*
- Step charts, *p86*
- Bubble charts, *p88*
- Picture tables, *p104*
- Heat maps, *p108*

x axis = horizontal axis
y axis = vertical axis

Figure 53 Vertical bar charts should always have baseline at zero (A). In a bar chart (B) with baseline at 1 item Y appears to be twice as big as item X, but it is in fact only 50 per cent bigger – as (A) makes clear.

Figure 54 A quantitative variable grouped in ranges becomes an ordered variable: there is a universal order between the four age ranges. Writing the labels on the horizontal scale on a 45-degree slant descending to the right combines space economy with easy reading.

Figure 55 The independent variable, kindergarten class (A), is categorical and can be reordered to show rank (B).

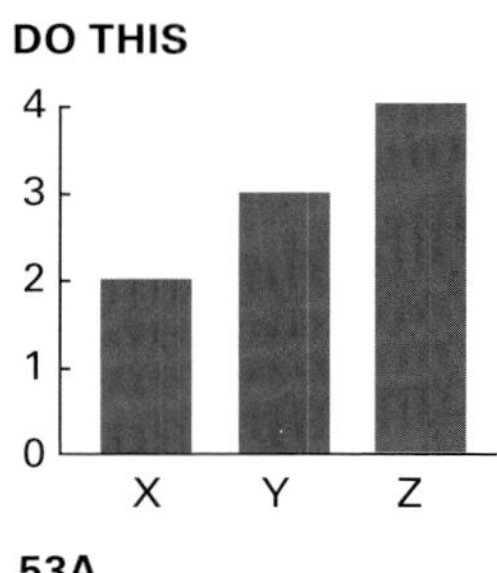

53A

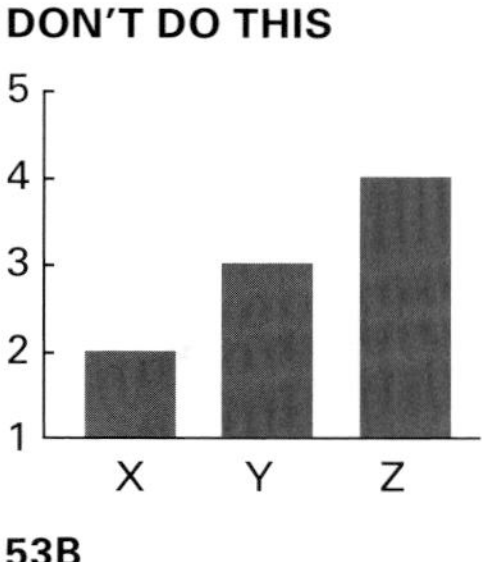

53B

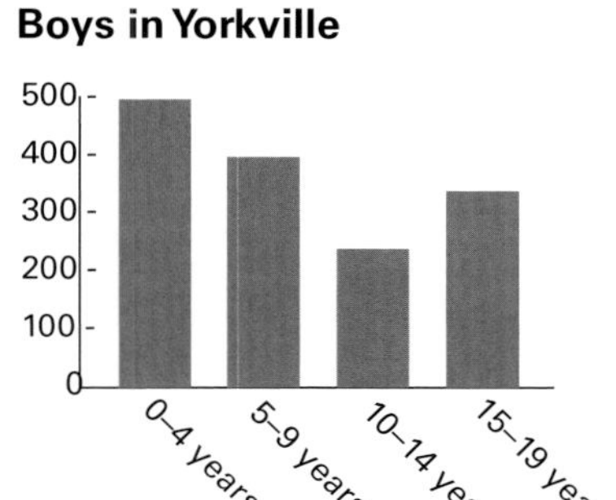

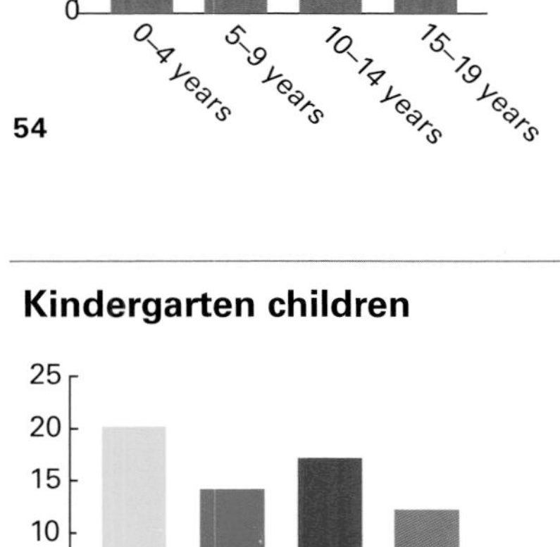

54

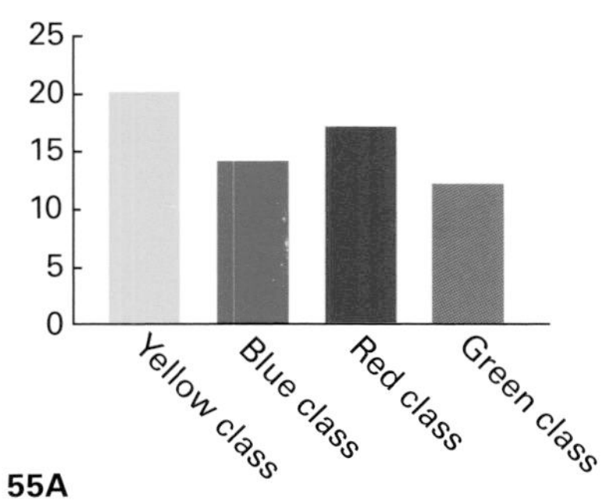

55A

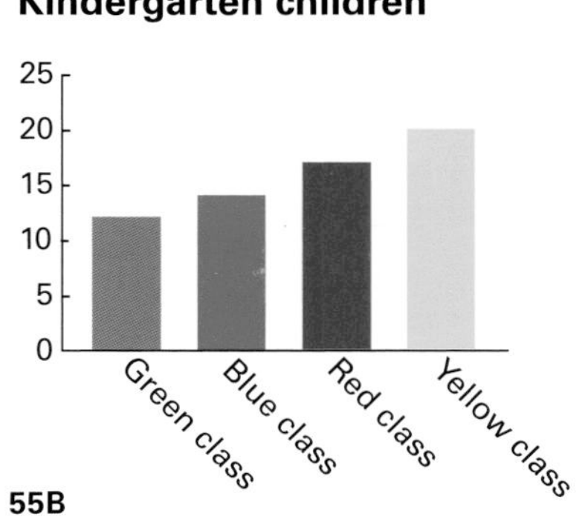

55B

Labels under the bars show the categorical or ordered scale of the independent variable. The quantitative scale of the dependent variable is shown on the left side of the vertical bar chart. Horizontal grid lines can be helpful.

If precise reading is important, the value of each bar can be shown directly, either inside or at the top of the bar. Values shown on the bars make the scale on the y axis redundant. It can be left out. However, the baseline should be kept.

If one bar requires visual emphasis, give it a different greytone or hue.

If the independent variable is showing ranges of time, and if there are more than five or six ranges, time could be treated as a continuous (quantitative) variable in a line chart *(see figure 61)*. While a bar chart enables elementary reading, i.e. reading the single correspondences, a line chart is better suited to enable overall reading, i.e. reading a trend.

Some designers use bubble charts instead of bar charts to compare the amounts of a small number of categories. Bubble charts have attention-capturing qualities but are inferior for precise reading *(see p88)*.

Figure 56 The quantitative scale to the left of the bars measures the dependent variable.

Figure 57 Horizontal grid lines *can* be helpful. They can be black or white.

Figure 58 Values on top of the bars make the scale on the y axis redundant.

Figure 59 If the independent variable (Australian states in this example) is categorical – without a given order – it can be rearranged to show rank.

Figure 60 Charts can emphasise one item by greytone (A) or hue (B).

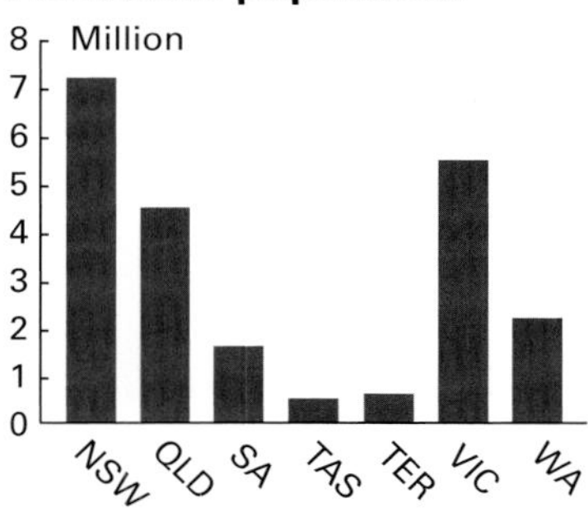

56

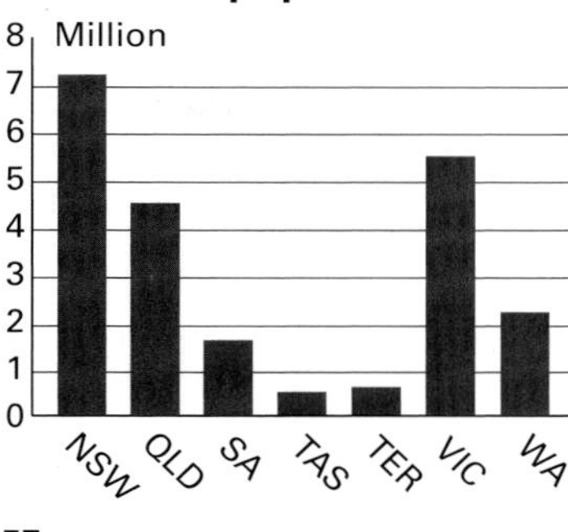

57

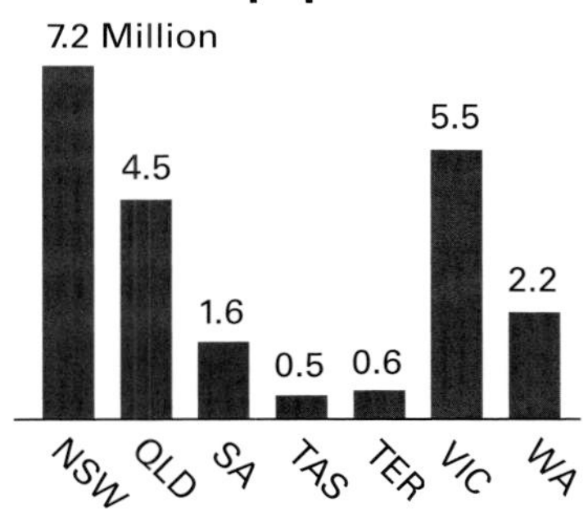

58

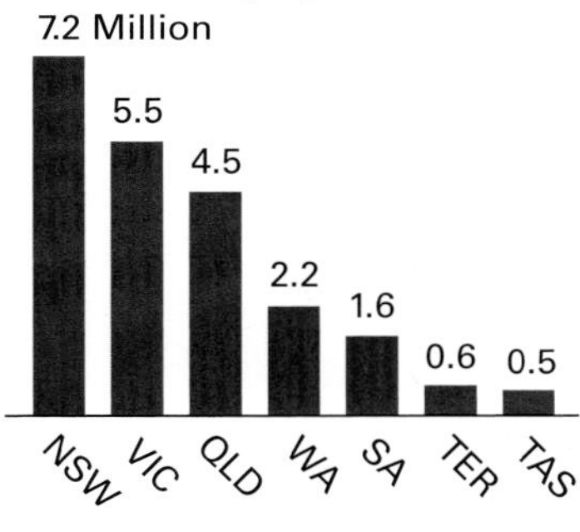

59

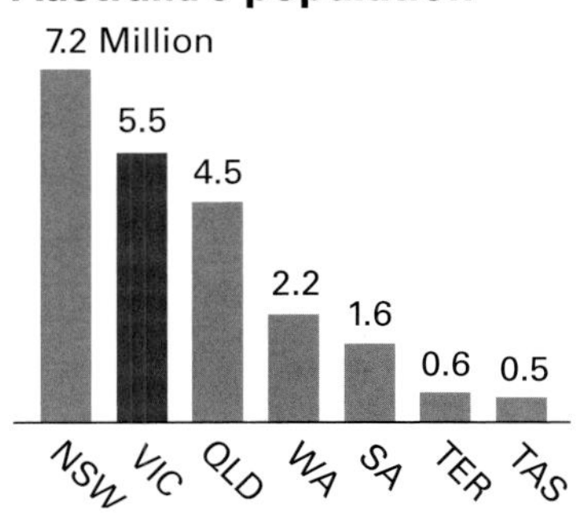

60A

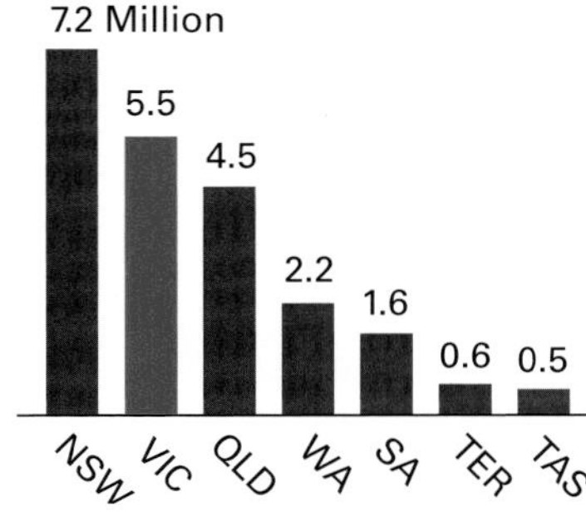

60B

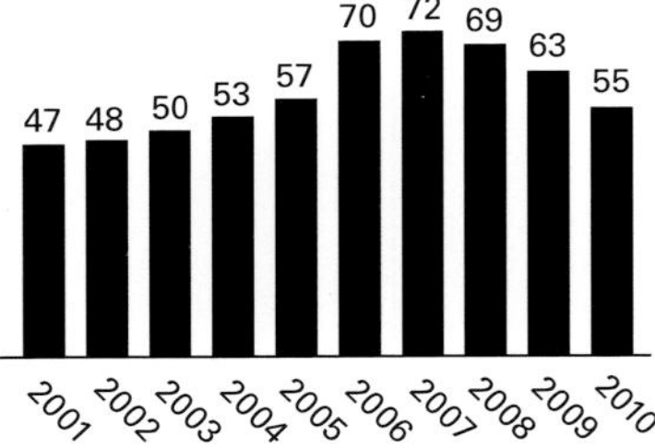

61A

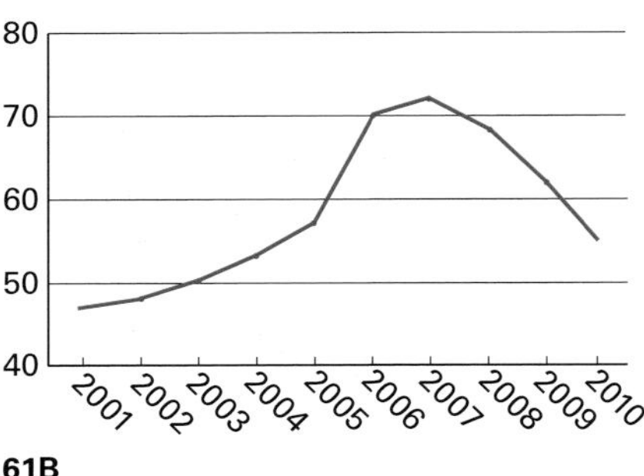

61B

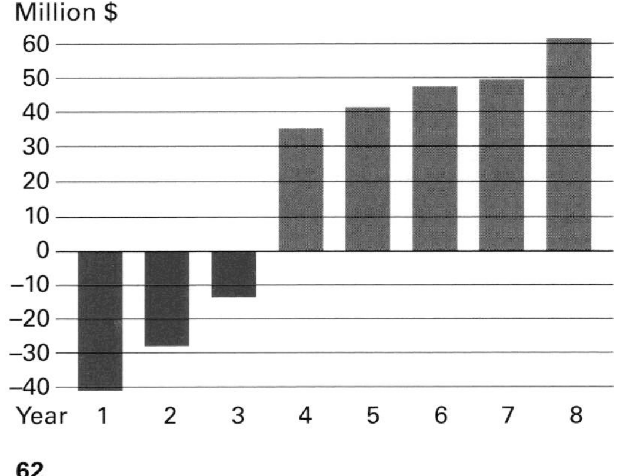

62

Figure 61 If a vertical bar chart represents ranges of time, and there are more than five or six ranges (A), and if the trend is more interesting than the values of the single years, a line chart should be considered (B).

Figure 62 In a vertical bar chart that shows financial results over a period, negative results can be shown under the baseline. Negative results can also be emphasised with greytone or red.

Figure 63 One vertical bar chart with multiple bars can substitute several bar charts.

Figure 64 Multiple vertical bar charts should not have more than three or four bars in each group. The bars in a group can be differentiated from each other by progressive greytone or colour.

Figure 65 If variation of measured values is relatively small as in (A), exact values may be interesting (B), and so may changes from year to year (C).

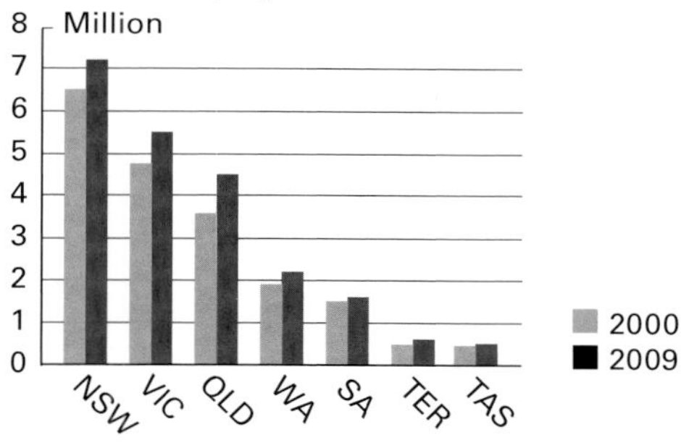

63

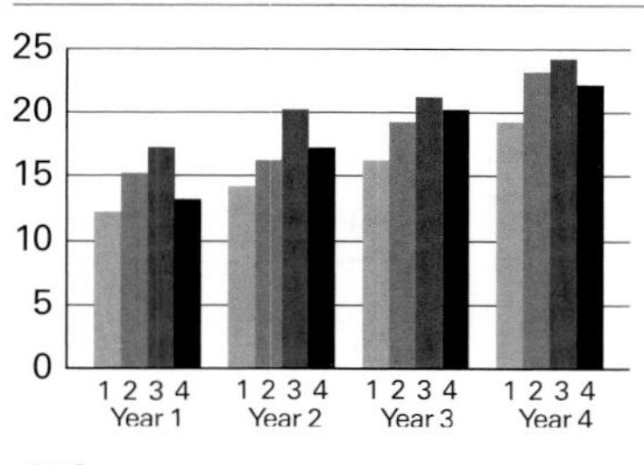

64A

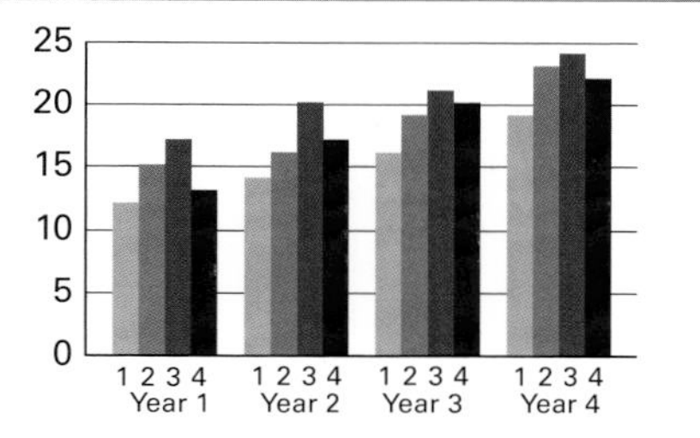

64B

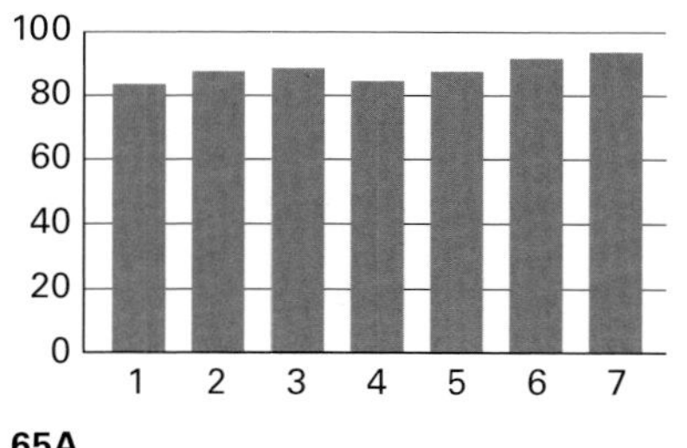

65A

83 87 88 85 87 91 93

1 2 3 4 5 6 7

65B

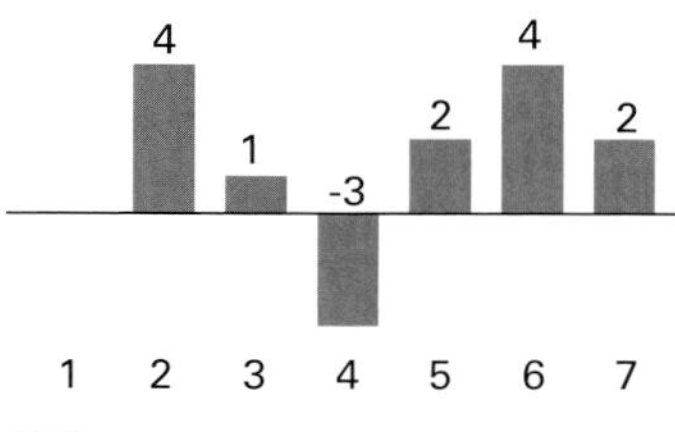

1 2 3 4 5 6 7

65C

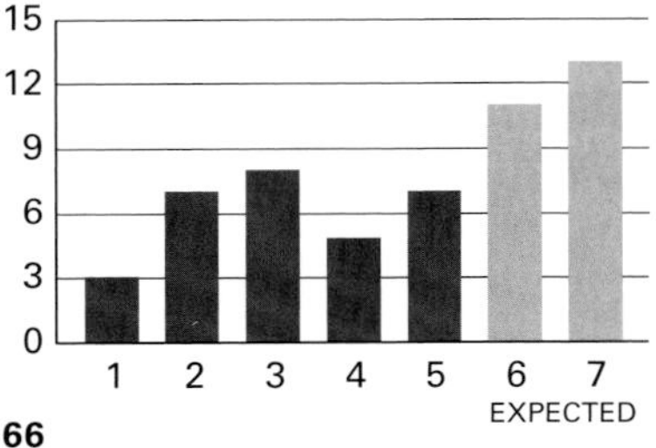

66

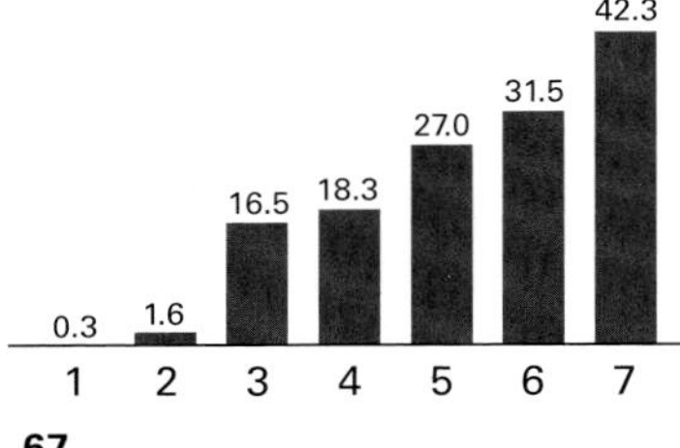

67

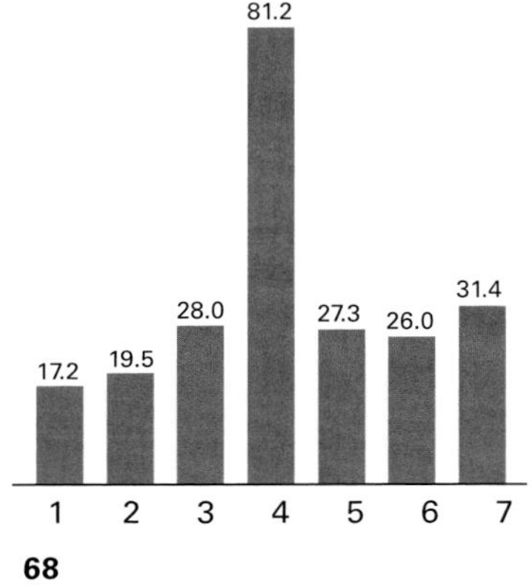

68

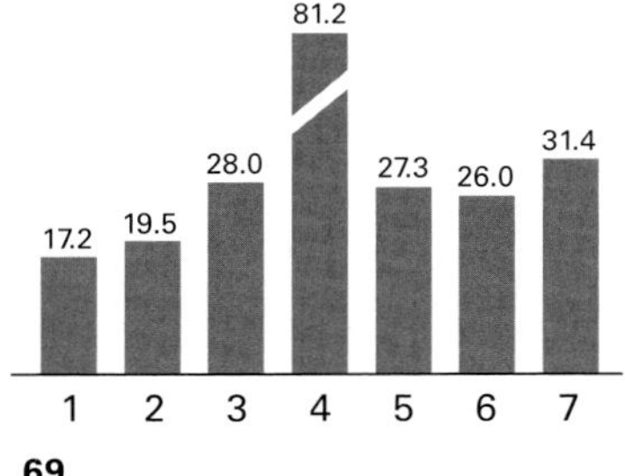

69

Figure 66 Expectations should be clearly distinguished from realised amounts by colour and by label.

Figure 67 Values too small to be shown as bars can be shown by figures.

Figure 68 Outliers, outstanding values, can capture attention.

Figure 69 Sometimes there is no space for outliers. Then one solution is a clearly marked broken bar.

Figure 70 Bar charts with too great a difference between the smallest and the greatest values can be a problem.

Figure 71 Data sets with a great difference between the smallest and the greatest values can be tamed by a logarithmic scale – if that is comprehensible to the intended audience.

Figure 72 This chart is both a vertical bar chart and a horizontal bar chart showing level of education and median income respectively. The height of the vertical bars shows the percentage of the Mexican population with one of six levels of education ranging from none to postgraduate education. The length of the horizontal bars shows the median monthly income of the six educational groups.
Data and design concept sourced from Centro de Estudios Espinosa Yglesias, Mexico www.ceey.org.mx/GMS/MS-00.html

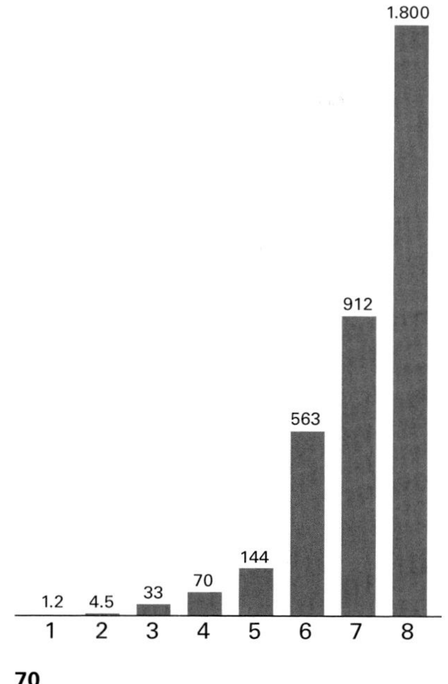

1.800
912
563
144
70
33
1.2
4.5
1
2
3
4
5
6
7
8

70

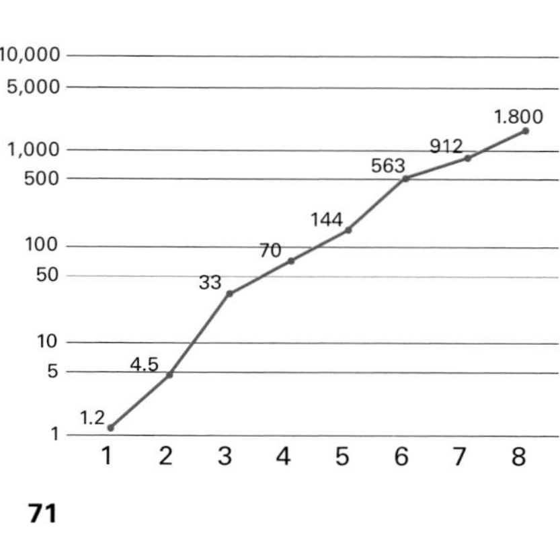

10,000
5,000
1,000
500
100
50
10
5
1
1.800
912
563
144
70
33
4.5
1.2
1
2
3
4
5
6
7
8

71

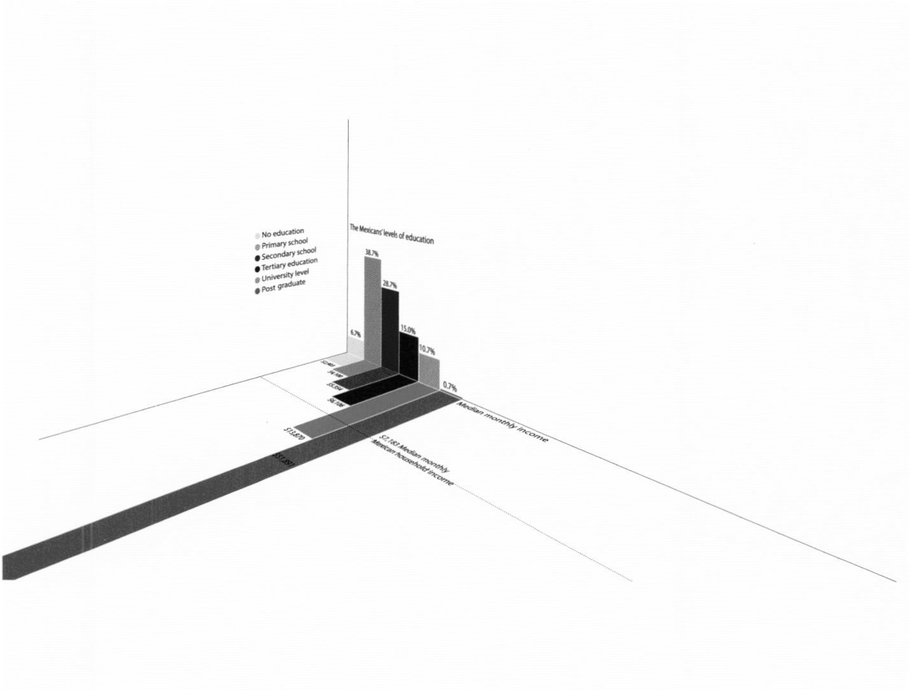

No education
Primary school
Secondary school
Tertiary education
University level
Post graduate
The Mexicans' levels of education
38.7%
28.7%
15.0%
10.7%
6.7%
0.7%
Median monthly income
$13,870
$7,183 Median monthly
Mexican household income

72

Histograms

How do ranges compare?

Histograms look similar to vertical bar charts, but they function differently. Histograms show values by the area of the bars, not by the height alone. In histograms, the bars are shown close to each other, without a horizontal distance.

Histograms are used to show distributions of continuous variables grouped in intervals, called *bins*. The bins are often equal, but can be of different size. The width of the bin multiplied with the height of the bar shows the frequency. The height alone (area divided by width) gives the relative frequency in a certain bin. Example: a bin of 0–4 years has a width of 5. If there are 42 hits in that bin, the height of the bar should be 8.4; it is the average number of instances per year in that bin *(see the table below and figure 73)*. If the values are shown as percentages of the total distribution, the total area will be 1 *(see the table below and figure 74)*.

Boys in Yorkville				
Bin	Number of boys	%	Average number of boys per year	Average % of boys per year
0–4	42	26.09	8.4	5.22
5–9	36	22.36	7.2	4.47
10–14	21	13.04	4.2	2.61
15–24	62	38.51	6.2	3.85
	161	100.00		

Other chart types that compare ranges include:
– Step charts, *p86*

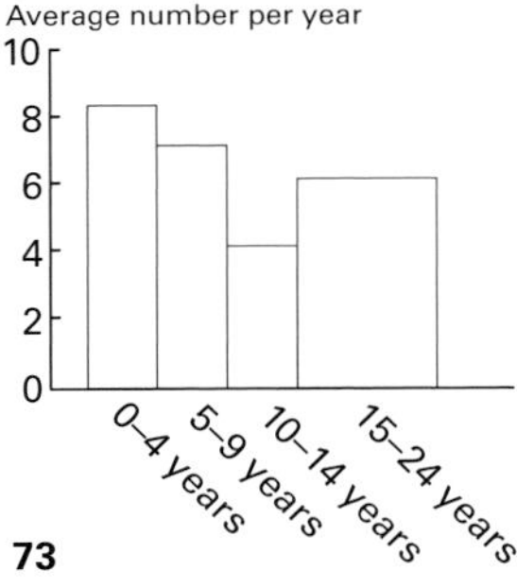

73

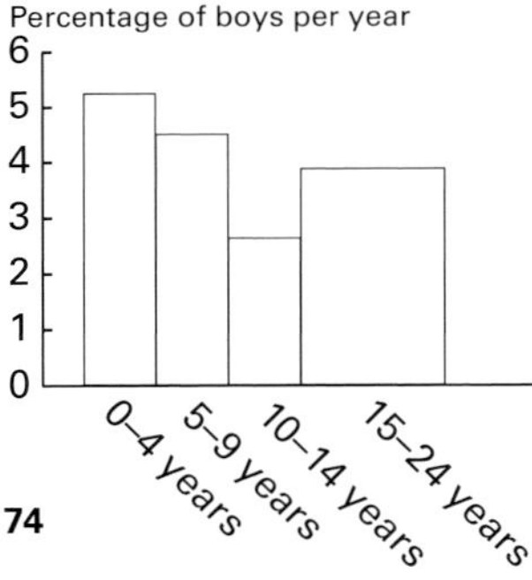

74

Figure 73 Histogram showing frequencies, numbers of instances in each bin (interval).

Figure 74 Histogram showing percentages of total number of instances in (73). The total area is 1.

Stem-and-leaf plots

How do ranges compare?

While the basic idea of visual displays is to substitute position, shape, size, and colour for raw figures, these figures may sometimes speak for themselves when organised appropriately. This happens in stem-and-leaf plots, where the first digits of instances form the stem, and the following digits make the leaves.

Both displays below visualise the following numbers, here presented in random order:

13, 27, 36 49, 58, 3, 62, 52, 76, 72, 20, 49, 36, 20, 64, 46, 36, 35, 35, 21, 41, 30, 82, 98, 16, 8, 15, 89, 74, 58, 12, 63, 71, 32, 23, 48, 55, 42, 57, 51, 61, 42, 40, 40, 34, 57, 58

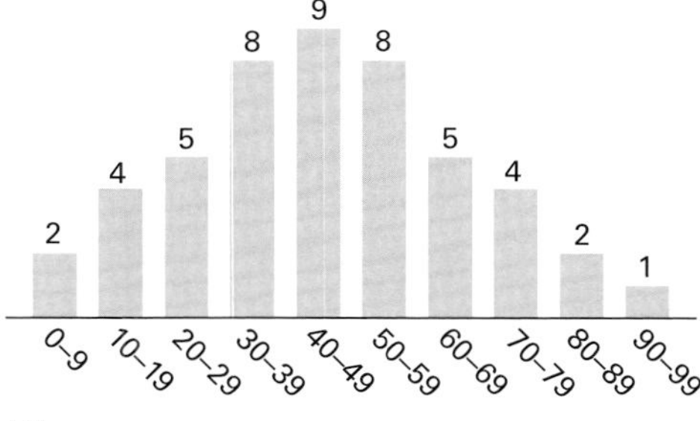

75

0	3 8
1	3 6 5 2
2	7 0 0 1 3
3	6 6 6 5 5 0 2 4
4	9 9 6 1 8 2 2 0 0
5	8 2 8 5 7 1 7 8
6	2 4 3 1
7	6 2 4 1
8	2 9
9	8

76

Figure 75 Vertical bar chart representing the numbers above. Instead of letting bars represent the figures, the figures could speak for themselves in a stem-and-leaf plot.

Figure 76 Stem-and-leaf plot representing the same data as figure 75. The figures on the left side of the red line are the first digits. The figures on the right side of the red line are the second digits of the instances. '4' in line '7' stands for '74'.

Horizontal bar charts

How do items compare in absolute amounts?
How do items rank?

Horizontal bar charts compare a limited number of relationships between an independent and a dependent variable. In contrast to vertical bar charts, horizontal bar charts have the independent variable along the y axis and the dependent variable along the x axis. The independent variable can be categorical or ordered. The dependent variable is quantitative.

In horizontal bar charts only the length of the bars signifies value, not the thickness. The thickness should be large enough to capture attention. All bars should have the same thickness. The vertical distance between the bars can be 50% of the bar thickness.

Labels to the left of each bar show the categorical or ordered scale of the independent variable. The quantitative scale of the dependent variable is shown under the horizontal bars. If precise reading is important, vertical grid lines can be helpful. Alternatively, the value of each bar can be shown directly on the bar, or at the right end of the bar. That makes the scale on the x axis redundant.

If the independent variable is categorical – not bound to a specific order – the bars can be reordered to show increasing or decreasing rank of competing teams, such as athletes, or research departments.

Don't make three-dimensional horizontal bar charts. They are difficult to read.

Horizontal bar charts are sometimes just called *bar charts* in contrast to column charts (vertical bar charts).

Other chart types that compare absolute amounts include:

- Vertical bar charts, *p68*
- Step charts, *p86*
- Bubble charts, *p88*
- Picture tables, *p104*

Figure 77 The quantitative scale under the bars measures the dependent variable.

Figure 78 Vertical grid lines *can* be helpful. They can be black or white.

Figure 79 Values at the end of the bars make the scale on the x axis redundant.

Figure 80 If the independent variable (here Australian states) is categorical – without a given order – it can be rearranged to show rank.

Figure 81 One bar can be emphasised by greytone or hue. The horizontal format allows longer labels on the categorical scale than vertical bar charts. Horizontal bar charts are sometimes chosen because of this quality.

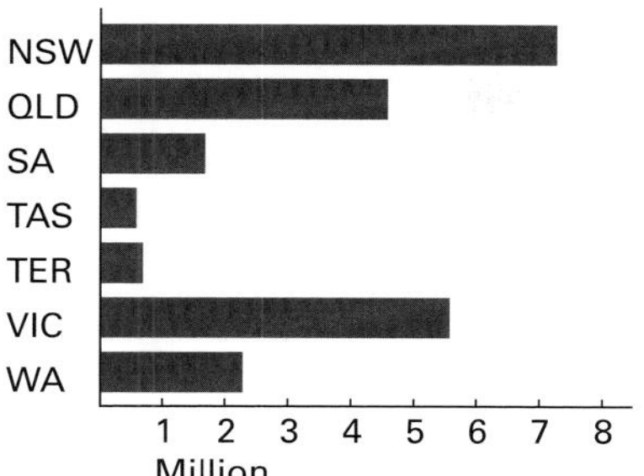
Australia's population
NSW
QLD
SA
TAS
TER
VIC
WA
1 2 3 4 5 6 7 8
Million

77

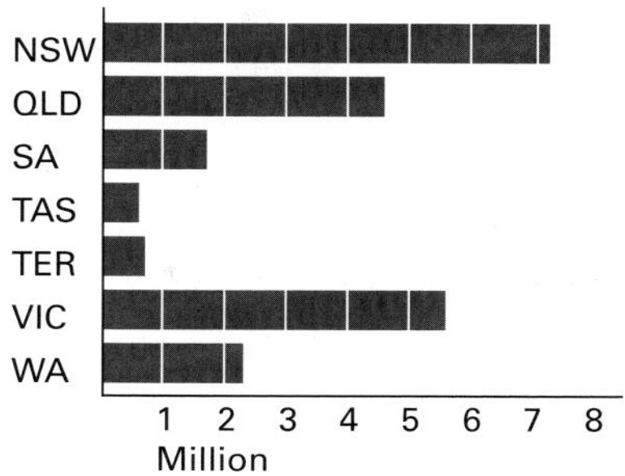
Australia's population
NSW
QLD
SA
TAS
TER
VIC
WA
1 2 3 4 5 6 7 8
Million

78

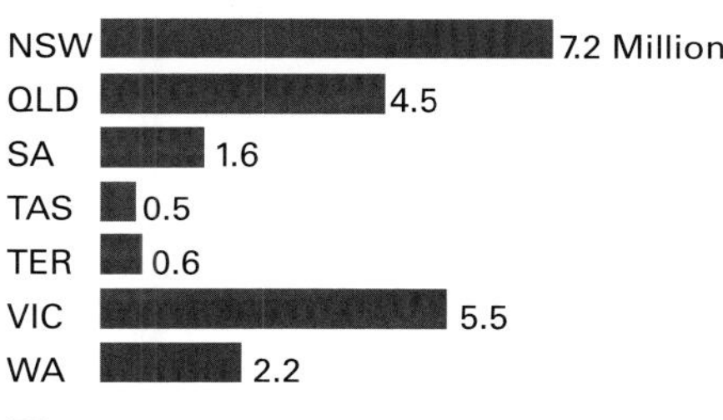
Australia's population
NSW 7.2 Million
QLD 4.5
SA 1.6
TAS 0.5
TER 0.6
VIC 5.5
WA 2.2

79

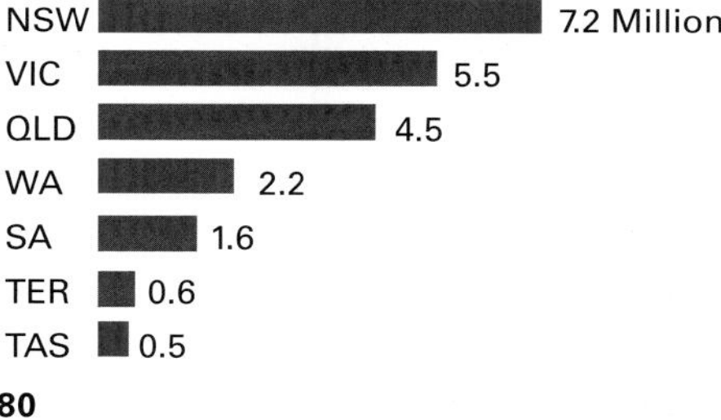
Australia's population
NSW 7.2 Million
VIC 5.5
QLD 4.5
WA 2.2
SA 1.6
TER 0.6
TAS 0.5

80

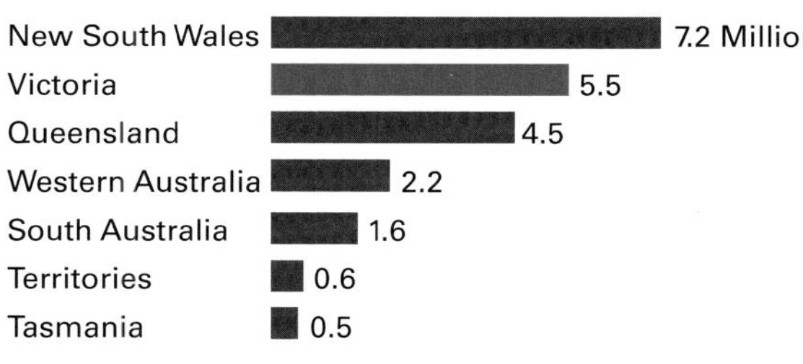
Australia's population
New South Wales 7.2 Millio
Victoria 5.5
Queensland 4.5
Western Australia 2.2
South Australia 1.6
Territories 0.6
Tasmania 0.5

81

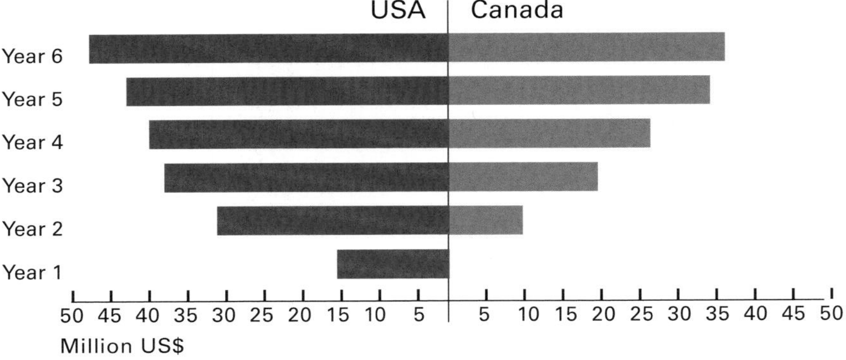

82

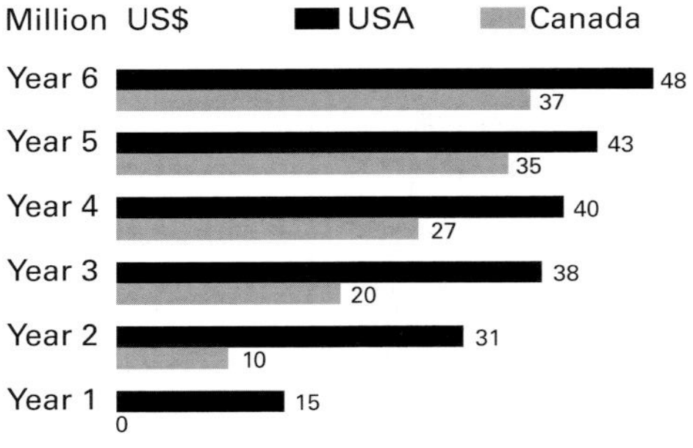

83

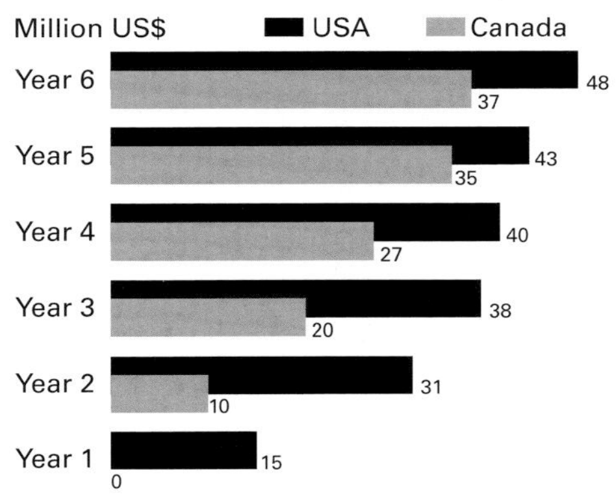

84

Figure 82 Side-by-side bar chart for comparing two dependent variables.

Figure 83 The same information as in (figure 82) shown in a less conspicuous multiple bar chart format that requires less space.

Figure 84 The overlapping multiple bar chart format is best when the values of the backmost dependent variable always are greater than the values of the foremost dependent variable.

Figure 85 A side-by-side bar chart that emphasises the difference between the two dependent variables.

Figure 86 A two-way horizontal bar chart format can also be used to show financial results.

Figure 87 Perhaps readers understand financial results faster in the usual format of a vertical bar chart than in a horizontal bar chart.

North American sales of product series

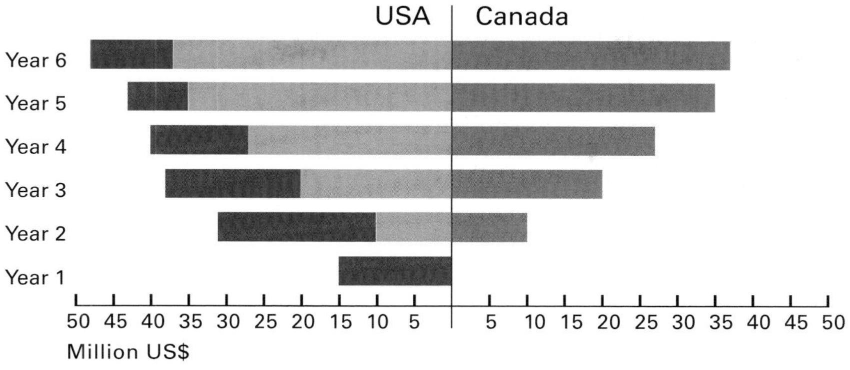

85

Introduction of new product

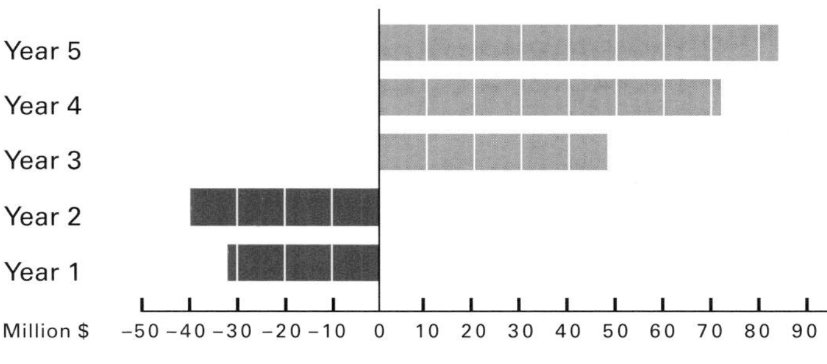

86

Introduction of new product

Million $

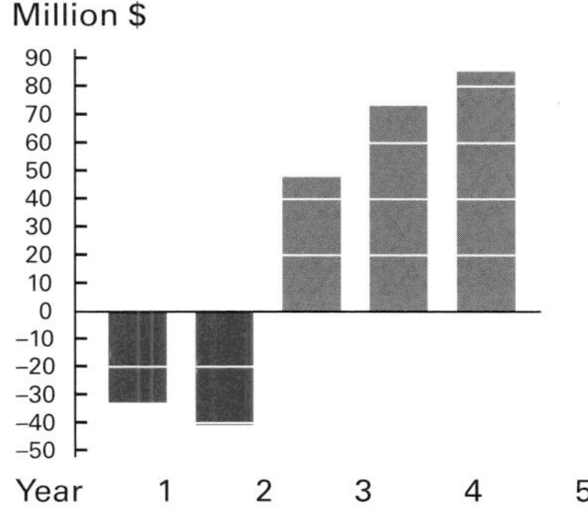

87

Divided-bar charts

How do parts of a whole compare with each other and with the whole?

Like pie charts, divided-bar charts divide a whole. In divided-bar charts the height of the bar is divided into percentage segments allowing quick comparison of the parts and the whole. The total height of the bar always amounts to 100 per cent.

Other chart types that compare parts of a whole include:
– Pie charts, *p60*
– Donut charts, *p66*
– Treemaps, *p149*

An independent and a dependent variable are both shown along the y axis. The independent variable represented by the bar segments is categorical or ordered. The dependent variable represented by the height of the bar segments is quantitative.

Labels that identify single segments can be shown to the right of the bar. If necessary, percentages can also be shown to the right of the bar. In contrast to pie charts, divided-bar charts can also show accumulated percentages. These can be shown to the left of the bar.

A divided-bar chart should not accommodate more than five or six parts. This is particularly important if several divided-bar charts are compared. If needed, a number of small parts can be grouped to meet this requirement.

When several divided-bar charts with the same types of parts are shown side by side for comparison, this implies introducing a new independent variable, categorical or ordered. This can be shown along the x axis with a label under each bar.

Figure 88 The simplest divided-bar chart.

Figure 89 Percentages can be added on a divided-bar chart if they are of interest to readers.

Figure 90 Accumulated percentages on a divided-bar chart can be added to the left of the divided-bar.

Figure 91 On a multiple divided-bar chart with great variation segments must be explained by a legend.

Figure 92 On this divided-bar chart one set of labels covers four divided-bars. Items such as "Yes", "No", and "Don't know" have a fixed order.

Figure 93 If one segment is of special interest, it can be explained in a new divided-bar chart. It is important not to use the greytones or hues already used.

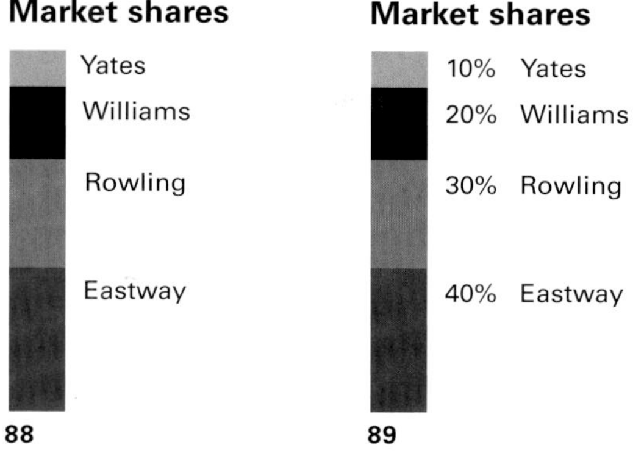
Market shares
Yates
Williams
Rowling
Eastway
88
Market shares
10% Yates
20% Williams
30% Rowling
40% Eastway
89

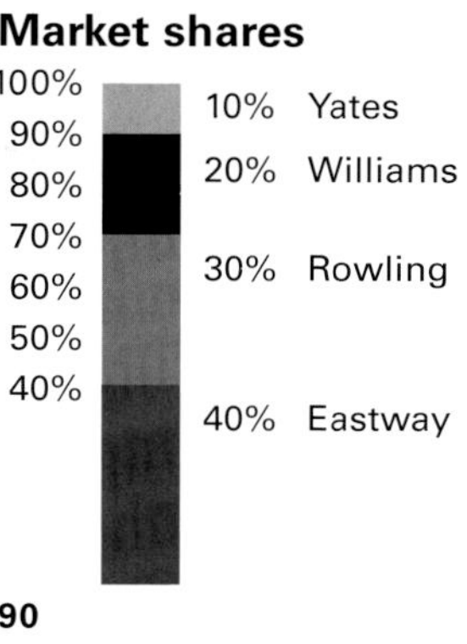
Market shares
100%
90%
80%
70%
60%
50%
40%
10% Yates
20% Williams
30% Rowling
40% Eastway
90

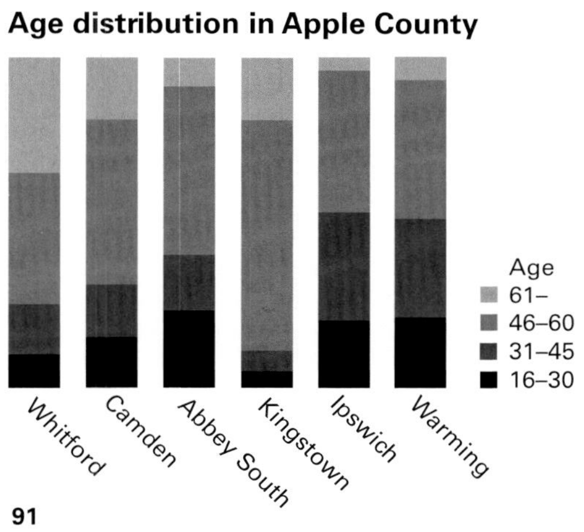
Age distribution in Apple County
Age
61–
46–60
31–45
16–30
Whitford
Camden
Abbey South
Kingstown
Ipswich
Warming
91

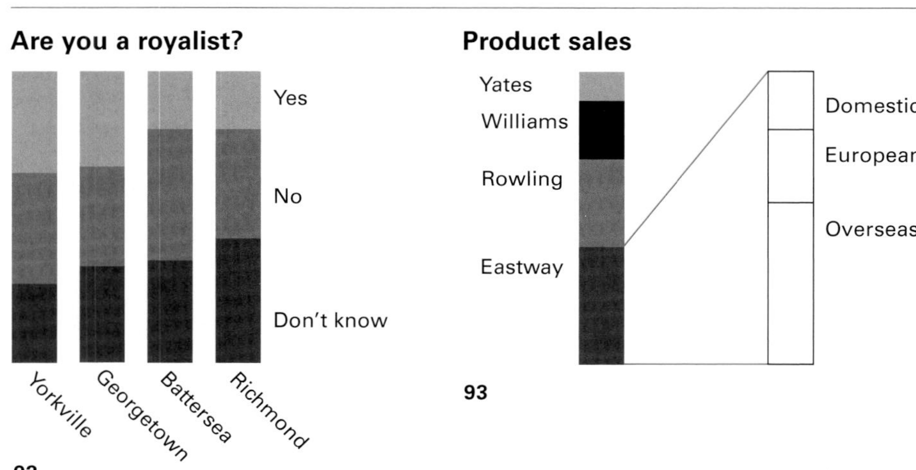
Are you a royalist?
Yes
No
Don't know
Yorkville
Georgetown
Battersea
Richmond
92
Product sales
Yates
Williams
Rowling
Eastway
Domestic
European
Overseas
93

Stacked bar charts

How do items compare with each other and accumulate?

In contrast to divided-bar charts, and pie charts, stacked bar charts compare absolute amounts, not percentages.

Other chart types that show aggregates include:
– Layer charts, *p96*

An independent and a dependent variable are both shown along the y axis. The independent variable represented by the bar segments can be categorical or ordered. The dependent variable represented by the height of the bar segments is quantitative.

Labels identifying the single segments – and if necessary their values – can be shown to the right of the bar. Stacked bar charts can also show cumulative values. These can be shown to the left of the bar.

When several stacked bar charts with the same types of segments are shown side by side for comparison, this implies introducing a new independent categorical or ordered variable, this time shown along the x axis with a label under each bar. The segments of the stacked bars should be shown in the same order in all stacks. A legend can identify the segments. A quantitative scale to the left of the display can help to make reading the chart easier.

Layer charts show the same type of information as stacked bar charts, but over time *(see p96)*.

Figure 94 A stacked bar chart can show both the total and amounts relating to the segments.

Figure 95 In multiple stacked bar charts a quantitative scale to the left can serve all bars.
If the bars are similar, labels to the right can serve all bars.

Figure 96 In case of great variation between the bars in a multiple stacked bar chart, a legend can identify the greytones or hues of the segments.

Figure 97 If there is no given order among the bar segments in multiple stacked bar charts the segment with the smallest variation can be placed at the bottom. This can make the legend redundant.

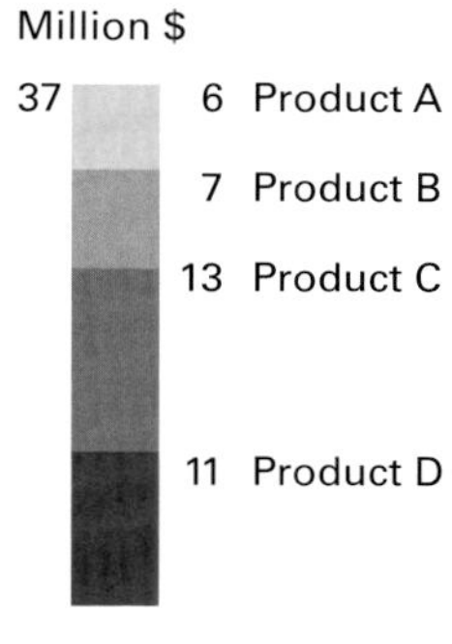
Sales of four products
Million $
37
6 Product A
7 Product B
13 Product C
11 Product D

94

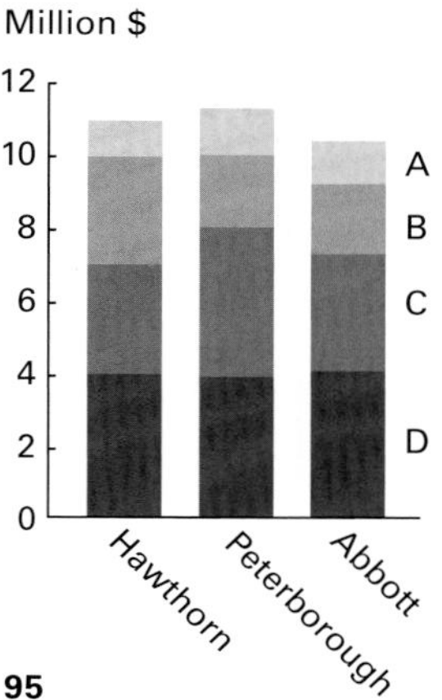
Sales of four products
Million $
12
10
8
6
4
2
0
A
B
C
D
Hawthorn
Peterborough
Abbott

95

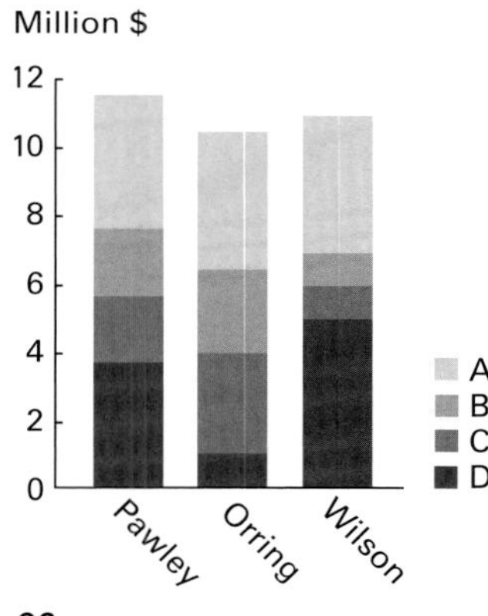
Sales of four products
Million $
12
10
8
6
4
2
0
A
B
C
D
Pawley
Orring
Wilson

96

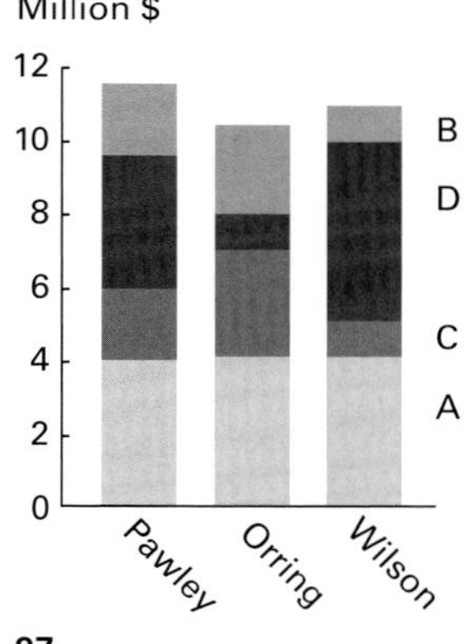
Sales of four products
Million $
12
10
8
6
4
2
0
B
D
C
A
Pawley
Orring
Wilson

97

Step charts

How do items compare in absolute amounts?

Step charts – vertical bar charts with no horizontal distance or vertical lines between the bars – are used to visualise quantitative variables with relatively few changes.

Other chart types that show range include:
- vertical bar charts, *p68*
- horizontal bar charts, *p78*

One typical use of step charts is seen when the independent variable is ordered showing time ranges of equal length, e.g. one year, or five years. The 'columns' of a step chart should – as in a bar chart – have equal width.

The labels of the independent variable should be placed under the 'columns' that form the steps.

A scale to the left of the steps can show the value of the dependent variable. The value of the dependent variable can also be shown on the top of each step. This enables a precise elementary reading.

If there are many steps in a step chart showing ranges, a line chart should be considered.

Figure 98 Step chart showing a time series with few measurements: the price of a public service.

Figure 99 Step charts can show a limited number of ranges, for example age groups.

Figure 100 Under special conditions, step charts can be used as a strong comparative display.

Passport fees 2005–2010

98

Boys in X-ville

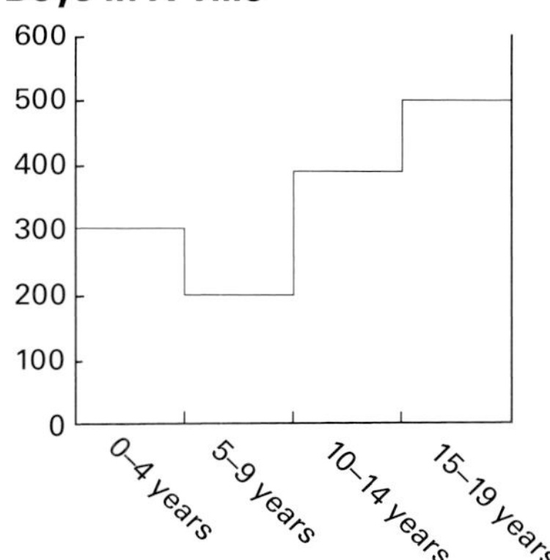

99

Prices compared

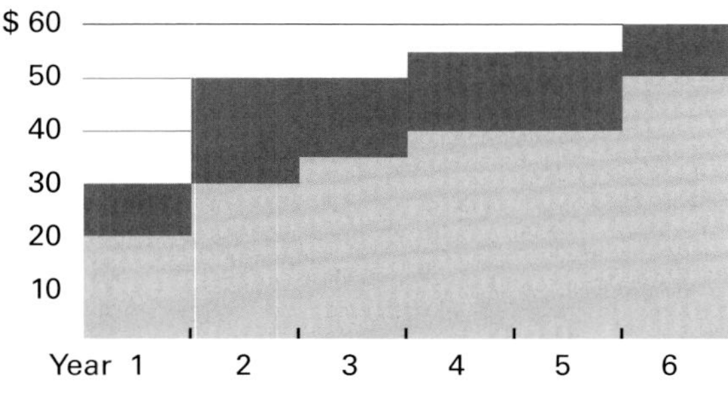

Competitor's price

Our price

100

Bubble charts

How do items compare in absolute amounts?
How do items rank?

Bubble charts do the same job as simple bar charts; they compare the values of a small number of items.

In bubble charts the bubbles represent the independent variable, which can be categorical or ordered. The area of the bubbles represents the dependent variable, which is quantitative.

Bubble charts are more attention grabbing than bar charts, but more difficult to read precisely. The areas of bubble charts are more difficult to compare than the heights of vertical bar charts. On top of that, readers may be in doubt whether they should read the diameter or the area of bubbles, for example the diameter, or the radius squared and multiplied with Pi (π): 6 or 3^2x3.141=28.27.

Bubble charts are popular because of their visual attraction. The main problem, however, remains: one-dimensional measures should preferably be shown in one dimension.

Bubble charts are also known as *disc charts*.

Other chart types that compare absolute amounts include:
- Vertical bar charts, *p68*
- Horizontal bar charts, *p78*
- Step charts, *p86*
- Picture tables, *p104*
- Heat maps, *p108*

See also bubbles used in:
- Scatter plots, *p100*
- Dorling cartograms, *p135*

Population in three cities

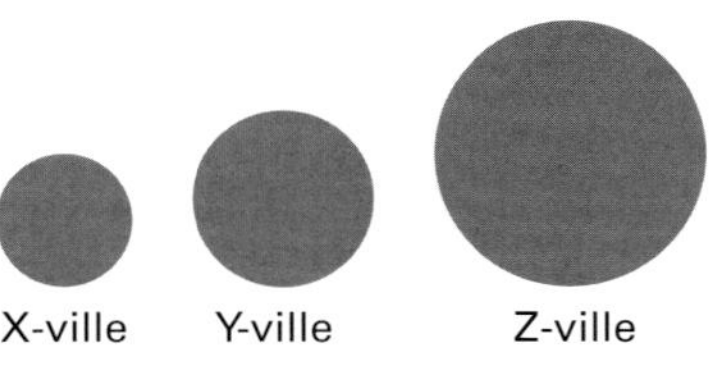

101

Figure 101 Readers may not know whether they should compare diameters or areas. Of course, the three bubbles can be labelled with values. Most bubble charts are equipped with numbers. They are hybrids.

Figure 102 Bubble chart with one independent variable: time, and two dependent variables: number of participants and turnover.

Figure 103 Walmart's revenues compared with other large US companies. Data and design concept sourced from *Co.Design* newsletter, published by Fast Company, US

Figure 104 Bubble chart ordered to show rank, and equipped with amounts in figures within the bubbles. Data source: http://www.worldometers.info/bicycles/

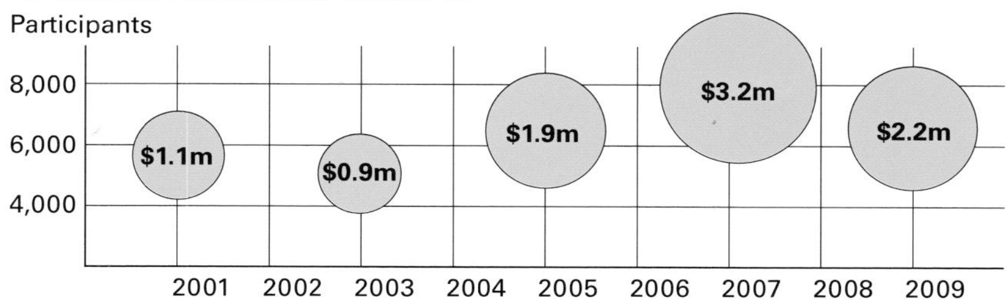

102

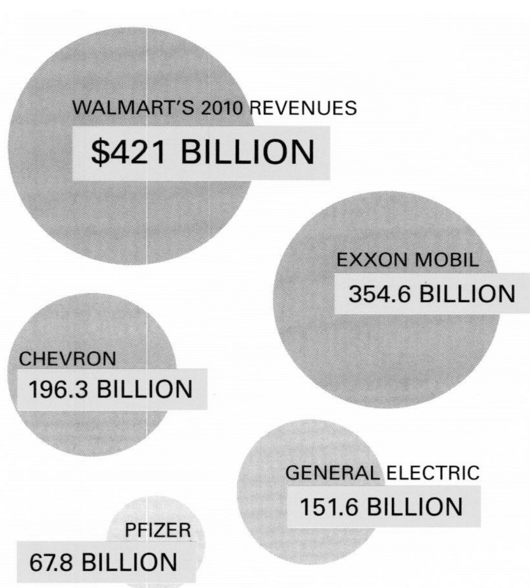

103

The world's five largest bicycle nations
Million bicycles

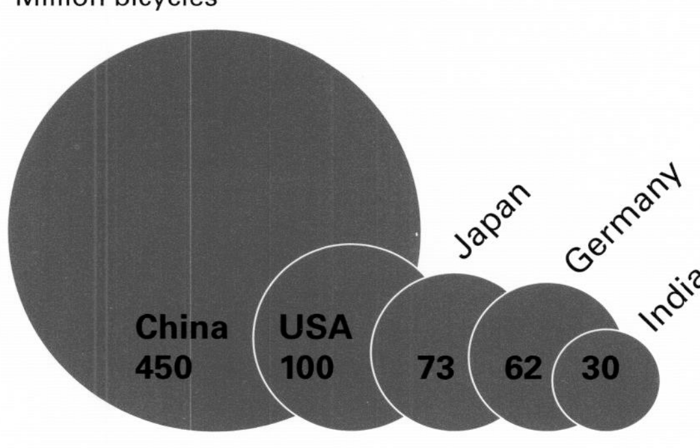

104

Line charts

How do one or more items vary with time or another continuous variable?

Line charts show correspondence between an independent quantitative variable and a dependent quantitative variable in a two-dimensional coordinate system. The independent variable and the dependent variable are shown along the x axis and y axis respectively. Line charts are typically used for time series, i.e. showing development over time.

Other chart types that show development over time include:
– Layer charts, *p96*

x axis = horizontal axis
y axis = vertical axis

Both axes of a line chart should have a clear numerical indication of scale. The baseline should be clearly marked, but does not have to be at zero. The non-zeroness of the baseline *can* be emphasised by breaking the y axis with a double slash or a zig-zag.

A grid of discreet, vertical and/or horizontal lines may help fast and precise reading.

A second independent, categorical variable, called a parameter, can be shown as two or three, rarely more than four, lines. In a line chart showing the development of urban traffic congestion, a parameter could be 'city', represented by lines for London, Paris, and Rome respectively. The lines can be distinguished by colour or texture.

Figure 105 Basic line chart showing a time series with one line.

Figure 106 Line chart with the same content (as figure 105), but with a truncated and stretched scale on the y axis to give a clearer picture.

Figure 107 Line chart with a second independent variable, gender. Direct labeling and colour coding help easy reading.

Figure 108 Line charts shouldn't have more than three or four lines representing instances of a parameter, preferably with direct labelling. When the lines mingle as they do here, a legend must replace direct labelling.

Figure 109 Same line chart (as figure 108) but with textured instead of coloured lines.

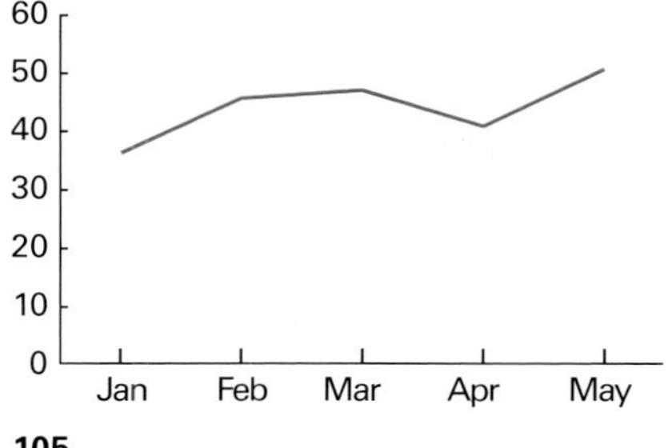

105

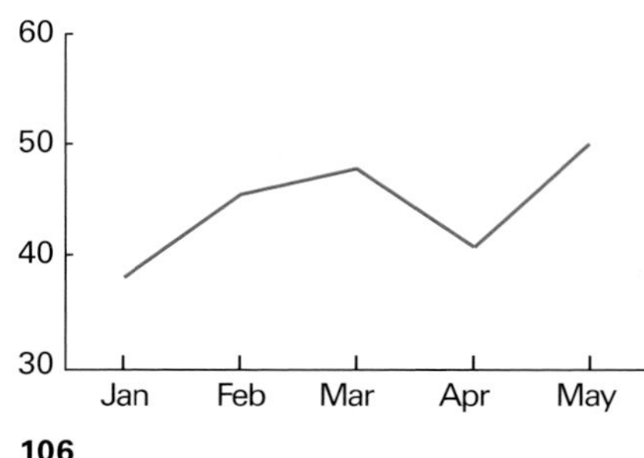

106

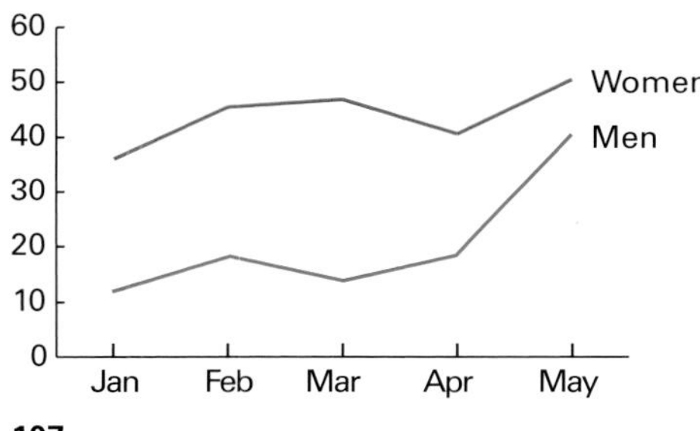

107

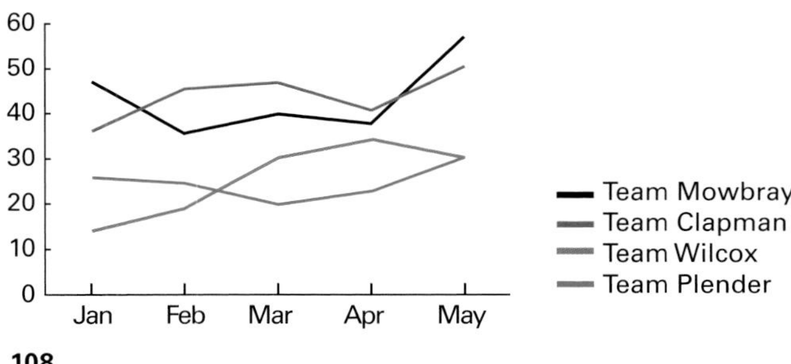

108

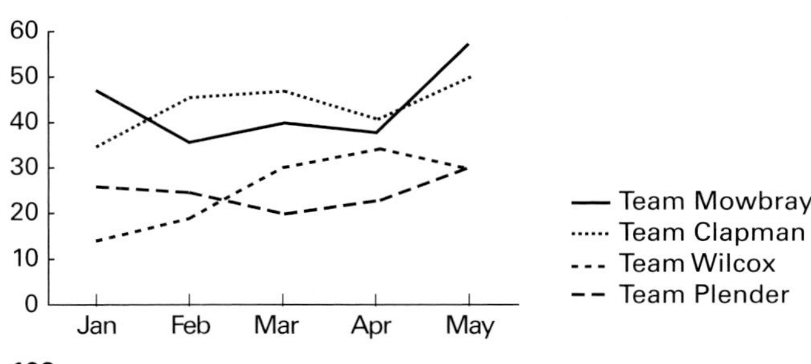

109

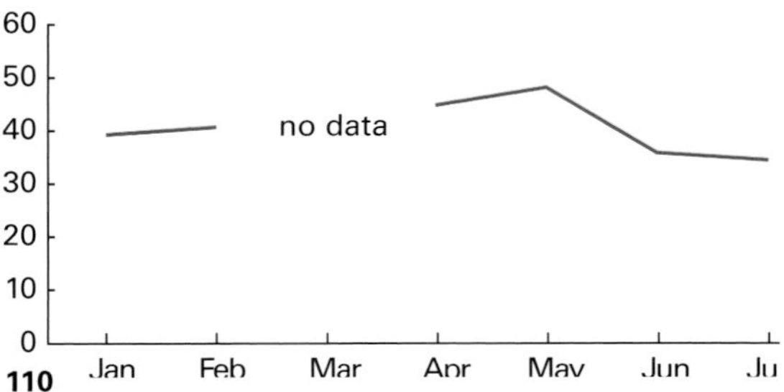

110

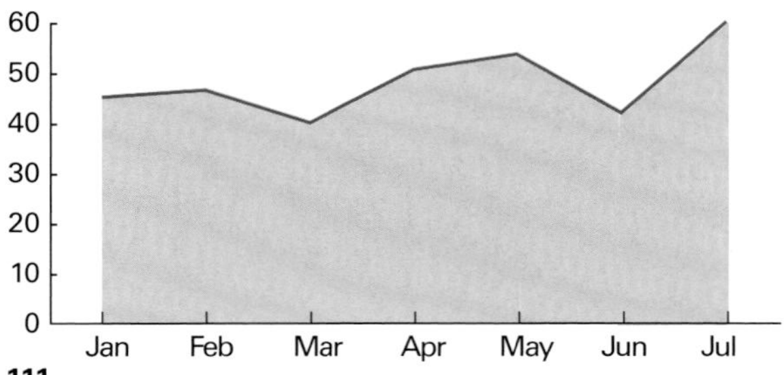

111

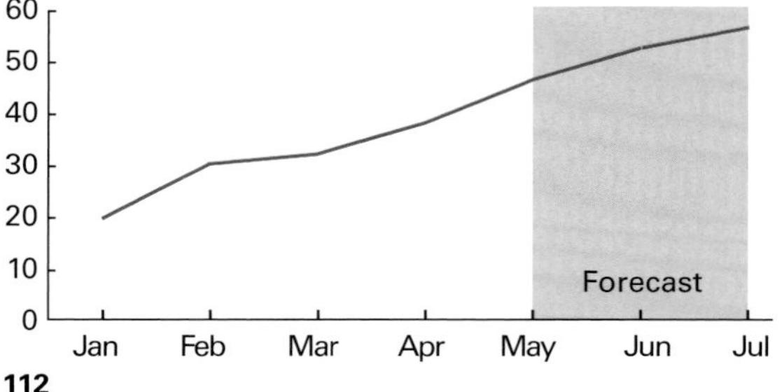

112

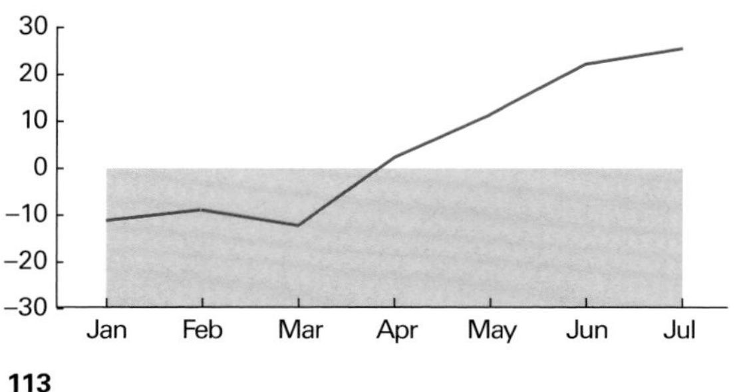

113

Figure 110 If some data are missing, this can be shown by a gap, perhaps explained by a label.

Figure 111 You *can* give the area under the line a shadow if the baseline is at zero.

Figure 112 Make forecast data clearly different from realised data.

Figure 113 A greytone can clarify the negative part of a scale.

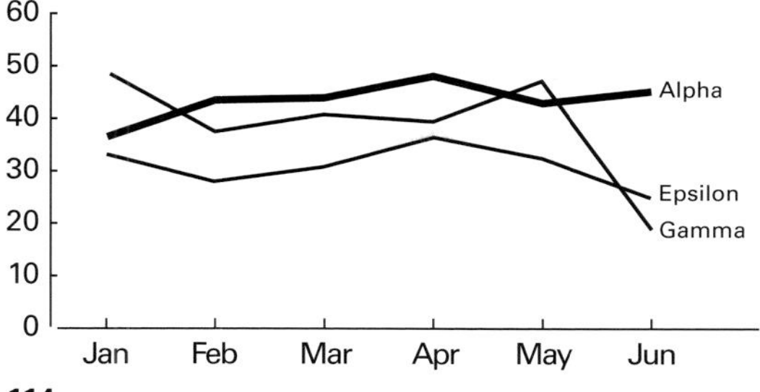

114

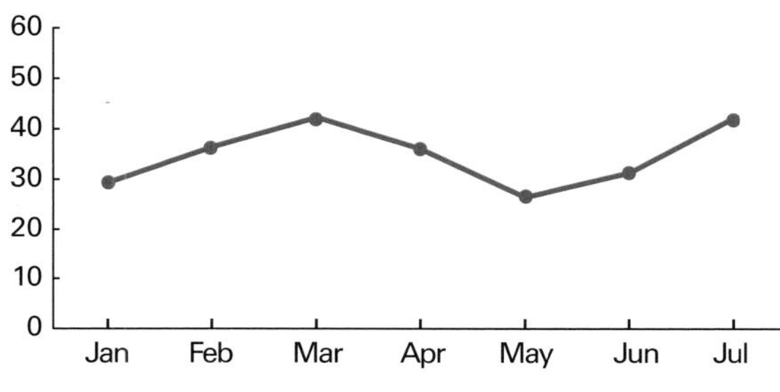

115

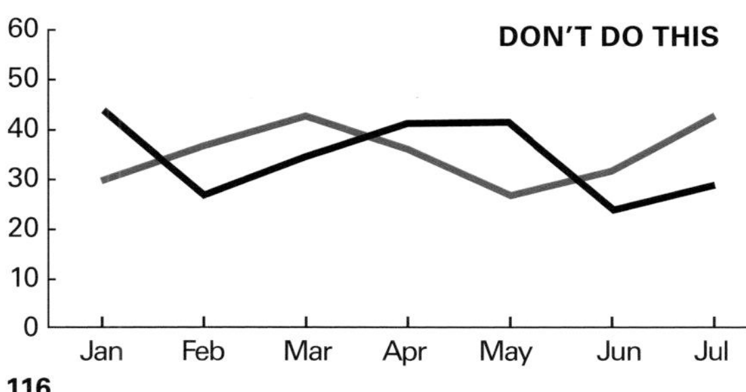

116

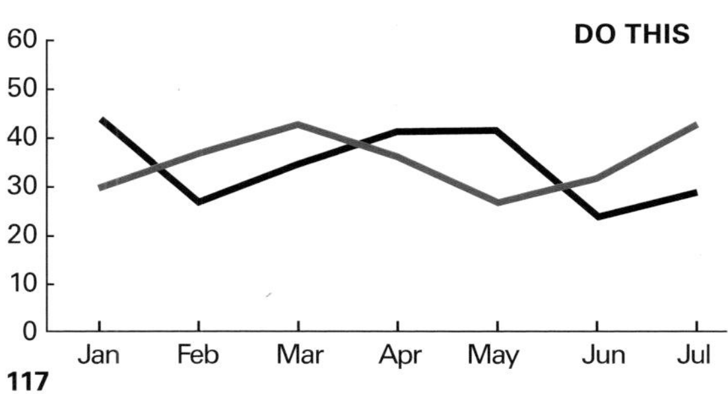

117

Figure 114 Emphasise when one line is more important than the other lines.

Figure 115 You *can* emphasise datapoints by dots.

Figure 116 Warm colours should be in front of cool colours. Don't let a red line go under a black line.

Figure 117 Let a red line go over a black line. It appears more natural.

Financial performance

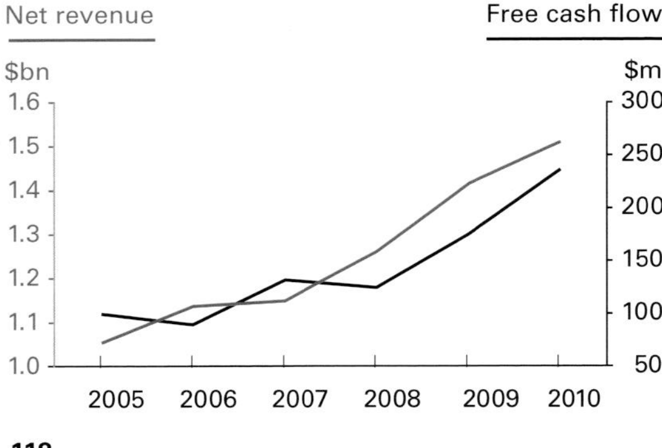

118

Gas price outruns the crude oil price

Index value

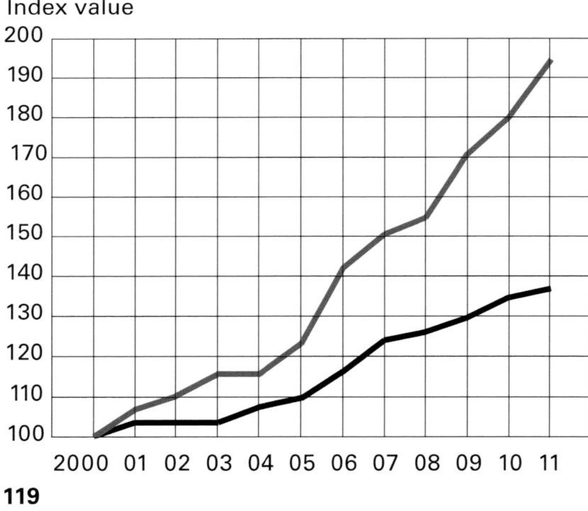

119

Delivery complaints

Number

%

60 50 40 30 20 10 0

100 90 80 70 60 50 40 30 20 10 0

Dept A B C D E

120

Figure 118 This display is a juxtaposition of two line charts, each with its own scale. The intent is to show covariation between net revenue and free cash flow.

Figure 119 Line charts given the right design can be strong visual arguments. High displays connote high prices. Here, the amounts are indexed with year 2000 as base.

Figure 120 The Pareto chart – named after Vilfredo Pareto, Italian economist – combines a vertical bar chart with a line chart that shows cumulative amounts. Pareto charts are sometimes used for quality control.

Figure 121 Annotated line chart where direct labels relate important incidents to changes in share price.

Figure 122 Line chart with another line chart detailing the most recent period.

Share prices during product introduction

121

Unemployment

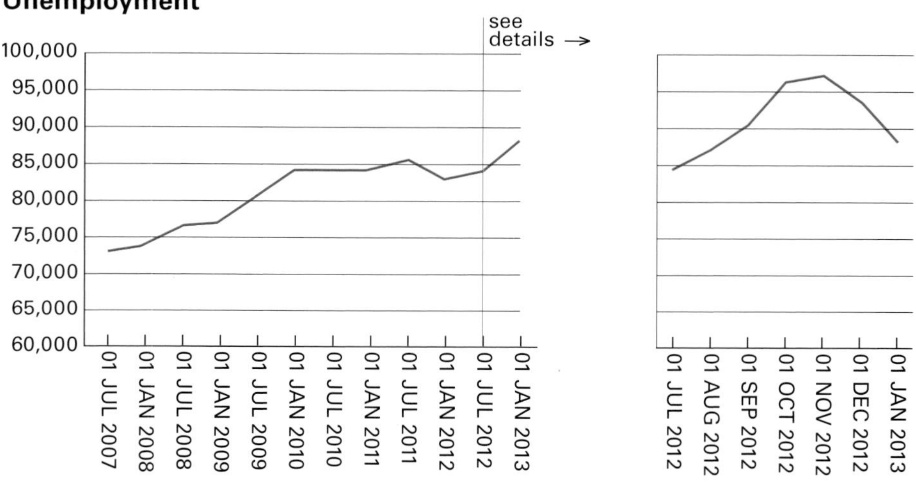

122

Layer charts

How do items that vary with time accumulate?

Layer charts are line charts stacked on top of each other to show a total. Time is the independent variable. Cumulative amounts are the dependent variable.

With a view to clarity, the number of layers shouldn't be greater than four or five. The layers should be clearly distinguished by shade or hue to make it completely clear that the layers are stacked on top of each other. Layers should be clearly labelled, directly if possible, otherwise identified by a legend.

If there is no natural order to the layers, clarity suggests that layers with the least variation should be placed at the bottom.

A layer chart can always be divided into a panel of individual line charts. However, this will not give the total, which can be shown in its own chart.

Layer charts are also known as *subdivided charts* and *area charts*.

Other chart types that compare cumulative amounts include:
– Stacked bar charts, *p84*

Other chart types that show development over time include:
– Step charts, *p86*
– Line charts, *p90*

Figure 123 Layer chart with four layers in random order (A). As there is no natural order between the layers they can be reordered with the layers with the least variation at the bottom (B).

Figure 124 The layers of figure 123 separated and shown in a panel.

Sales promoters' performance

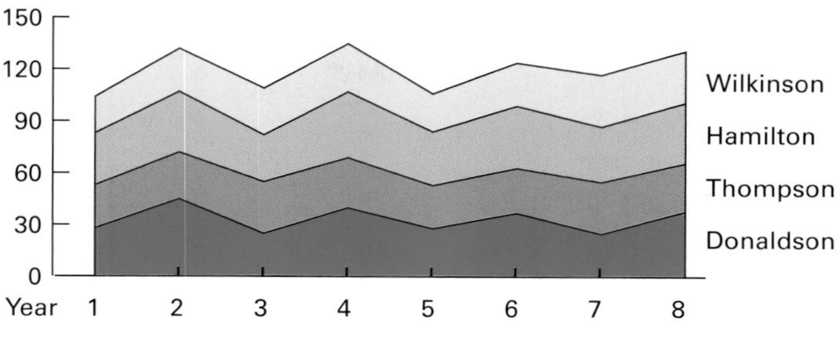

123A

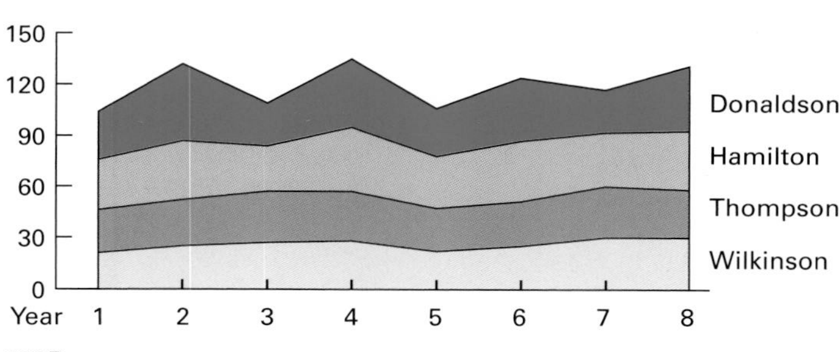

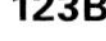

123B

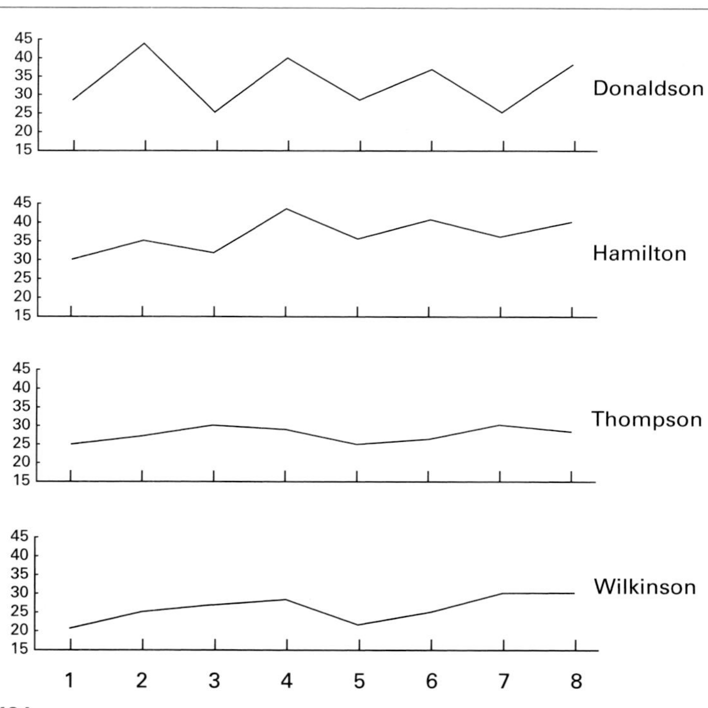

124

Radar charts

How do items vary with a factor and compare?

Radar charts are also known as *web charts*, *spider charts*, and *star charts*.

Radar charts compare a limited number of relationships between an independent variable and a dependent variable.

Radar charts deal with the same type of questions as bar charts. However, the polar form of the radar chart gives an impression of wholeness and invites cyclical data such as hours, days, and months.

The independent variable is shown as spokes, radii. This variable is typically ordered to represent, for example, weekdays or months. It can also be categorical, representing, for example, business units. The dependent variable is shown along the spokes. It is quantitative. A line connecting datapoints on the spokes provides overview and gives the chart the memorable form reflected in the name.

Lines of different hues or textures connecting the data points can represent a second independent variable. If the first independent variable represented by the spokes is weekday, the second independent variable can, for example, be the way hours are spent with work, leisure, and sleep.

Florence Nightingale designed her own radar-like polar chart to show the causes of mortality during the Crimean war *(see pp24/25)*.

Figure 125 Radar chart with month as independent variable shown as spokes and occupancy in percentages as the dependent variable measured along the spokes.

Figure 126 Radar chart with month as one independent variable shown as spokes. Sun movement is another independent variable, a parameter with two instances: sunrise and sunset. Sun movement is shown along the spokes. Hour is the dependent variable. It is shown along the spokes. The outer areas defined by the datapoints are shaded to emphasise the day and night pattern.

Figure 127 Radar chart with leadership quality as an independent variable shown by the spokes. The candidate is another independent variable with two instances, Anderson and Berghof. They are shown along the spokes. Accomplishment is the dependent variable represented along the spokes. The measurements on the spokes are connected with coloured lines that enable easy reading.

Mountain hotel sales

% occupancy

JAN FEB MAR APR MAY JUN JUL AUG SEP OCT NOV DEC

20 40 60 80 100

125

Sunrise and sunset, Copenhagen

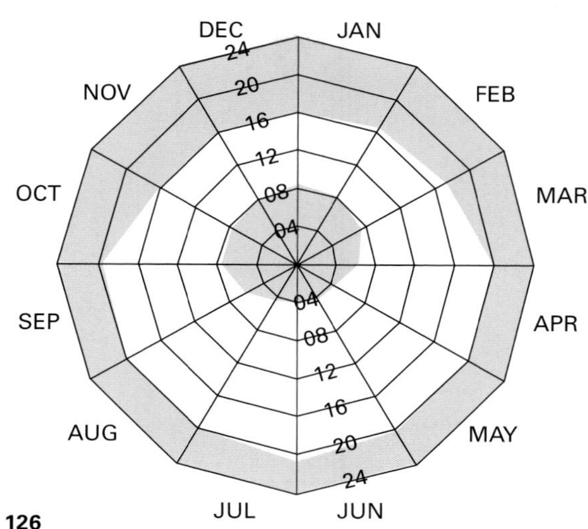

126

Comparing two CEO candidates

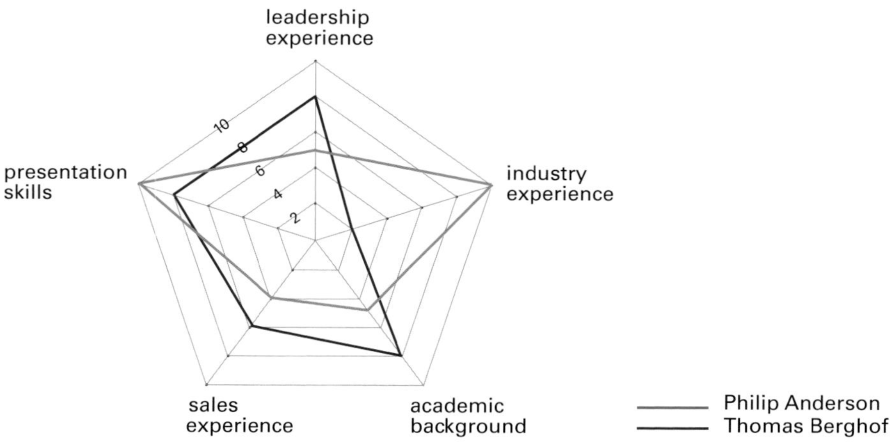

127

Scatter plots

How do two quantitative variables correlate?

Scatter plots are also known as *scatter graphs* and *scattergrams*.

Scatter plots show the correspondence between two variables as points in a two-dimensional Cartesian coordinate system. The two variables are shown along the x and y axis respectively.

An oblong pattern of points from lower left to upper right indicates a positive correlation. An oblong pattern of points from upper left to lower right indicates a negative correlation. If there is no clear pattern, there is no correlation.

A line can be drawn through the oblong pattern of a scatter plot (with correlation) to show the trend. Statisticians have mathematical methods to draw the best-fit trend. They can also calculate a measure of the correlation.

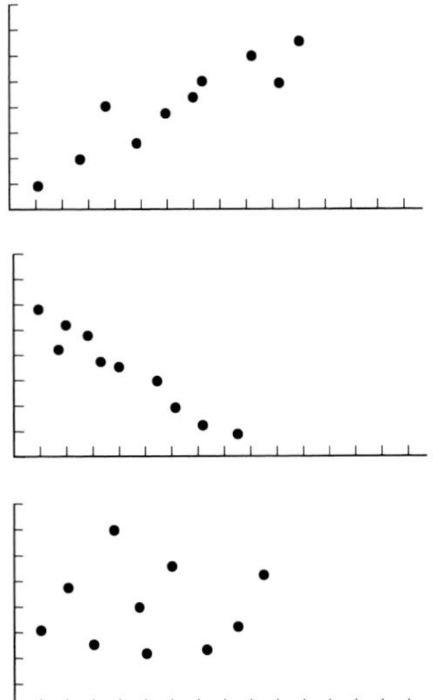

128

Figure 128 Three scatter plots with strong positive, strong negative, and no correlation, respectively.

Figure 129 A scatter plot with no strong correlation also tells a story: No, the oldest employees are not those with most sick days.

Figure 130 An informative scatter plot showing the correlation between average income per person and life expectancy in years shown along the x and y axis respectively. The positions of the bubbles serve as datapoints in a normal scatterplot. The sizes of the bubbles tell the population sizes. Finally, the colours of the bubbles tell the geographical region. The strong pattern along the diagonal suggests a strong correlation between income and life expectancy. Source: www.gapminder.org/world

Average sick days per year in customer service

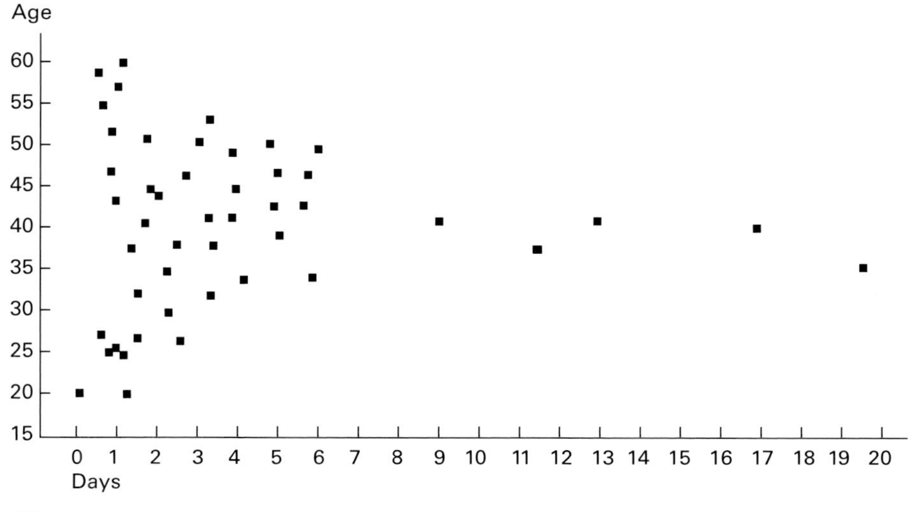

129

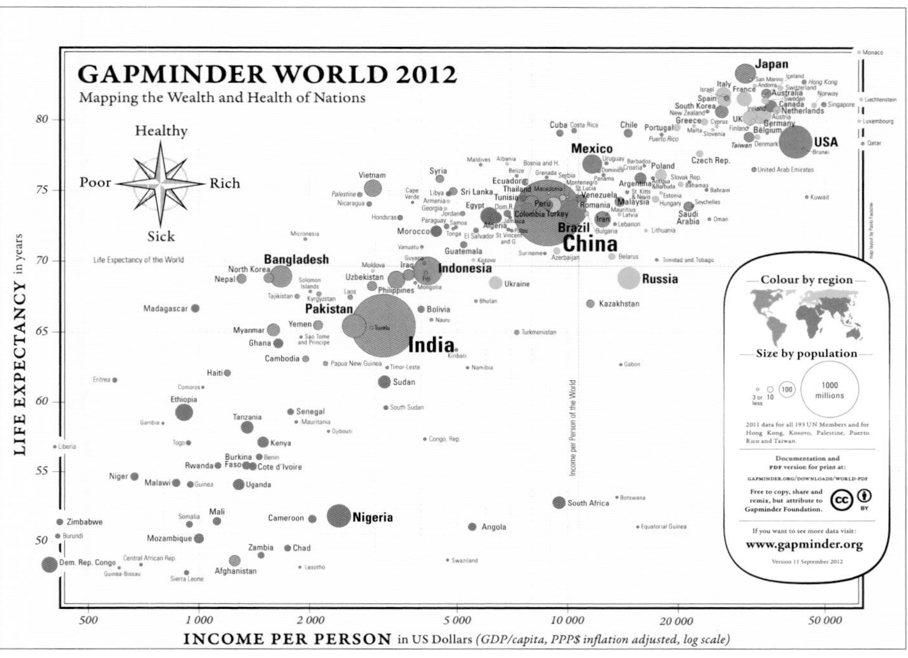

130

Slopegraphs

How does a quantitative variable change over a fixed period?

Edward R. Tufte used slopegraphs* to look at a single variable over a fixed period of time. In Tufte's original example he looked at receipts of government as a percentage of gross domestic product in selected nations 1970 and 1979. Nation and time are independent variables, government receipts are the dependent variable. The datapoints are shown on two parallel quantitative scales. They also show rank. The entries on the two parallel scales are connected with lines. The slopes of these lines tell an important part of the story:

- How does the single item change over time?
- How do the changes (slopes) of different items compare?
- What is the general trend?

Each line in a slopegraph would be a point if the data were shown in a scatter plot with the two years shown as axes. The benefit of using more ink in the slopegraph is the clear picture where parallel and almost parallel lines show what in the scatter plot would have been datapoints along a diagonal. Atypical slopes in a slopegraph would be datapoints away from the diagonal in a scatter plot.

While slopegraphs in Tufte's format deal with one variable over time, a similar type of display can show covariance between two or more variables over several periods.

Edward R. Tufte
The Visual Display of Quantitative Information, Graphics Press, Cheshire, Connecticut, 1983, 2001

*Originally, Tufte called these displays *table-graphics*, but later changed the name to *slopegraphs*.

Figure 131 Slopegraph. Data and design concept sourced from Edward R. Tufte, *The Visual Display of Quantitative Information, pp158/159*

Current Receipts of Government as a
Percentage of Gross Domestic Product
1970 and 1979

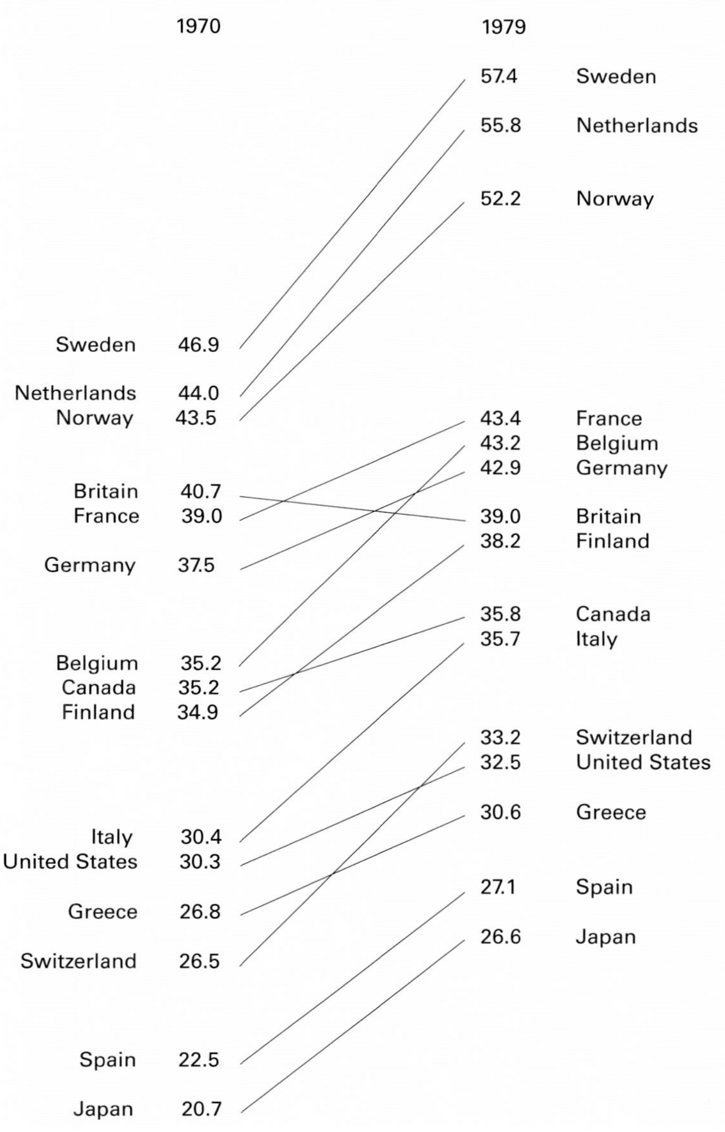

131

Picture tables

How do items compare?
How do items rank?

Picture tables are visual displays with rows of the repeated picture symbols as suggested by Isotype *(see pp30–33)*.

Most picture tables are scaled: each symbol stands for several real-world units, perhaps one hundred, one thousand, or one million. In unscaled picture tables, each picture stands for one real-world unit.

The independent variable, shown in rows, sometimes stacks of rows of pictograms, is categorical. The dependent variable, shown as numbers of pictograms, is quantitative.

Picture tables do not give faster or more precise information than sheer numbers. No matter how well organised in neat rows of equal length they are, it takes some time to count the symbols in a row, count the number of rows, and multiply the number of pictograms in a row with the number of rows. Extra time is needed, if the display shows a number of complete rows plus a fraction of a row and a fraction of a pictogram. Even more time is needed if the table is scaled: the scaling factor must be found, read, and multiplied with the result of the counting to calculate the final quantities.

Picture tables are first and foremost a means of visual attraction. Other display formats can do the same technical job with less ink and faster and more precise reading.

Figure 132 Unscaled picture table as rhetoric: Casualties after attacks on Oslo and the Norwegian island Utøya 21 July 2011. The black crosses representing the casualties of the massacre tell their tragic story. (The number of casualties later proved to be 77, not 92.)
Politiken, DK, 24 Jul 2011

Picture tables capture and hold the attention, and they are memorable. Also, perhaps most important, picture tables can provide strong rhetorical arguments. It is easier to read the number 92 than to count nine lines each with ten black crosses and one line with two black crosses, but the display of 92 black crosses each standing for a casualty is strongly argumentative: this is cruel.

Søndag

24. juli 2011
Årgang 127. Nr. 293
Pris 25,00
Kundecenter
Politiken 70 15 01 01
1. udgave
www.politiken.dk

i vandet omkring de unges ø

POLITIKEN MENER

Norge

† † † † † † † † † †
† † † † † † † † † †
† † † † † † † † † †
† † † † † † † † † †
† † † † † † † † † †
† † † † † † † † † †
† † † † † † † † † †
† † † † † † † † † †
† † † † † † † † † †
† †

I dag står billedet klarere. Smerten, sorgen, tragedien. Nu kender vi omfanget, målet, meningsløsheden. Vi ved, at flere end 90 mennesker er dræbt, flere såret. Langt de fleste er unge, der var på politisk sommerlejr organiseret af det norske Arbeiderparti. Det er næsten ubegribeligt. Og alligevel nu en del af vores fælles virkelighed. En erfaring, vi må lære at håndtere, forstå og leve videre med: Det kan ske.

132

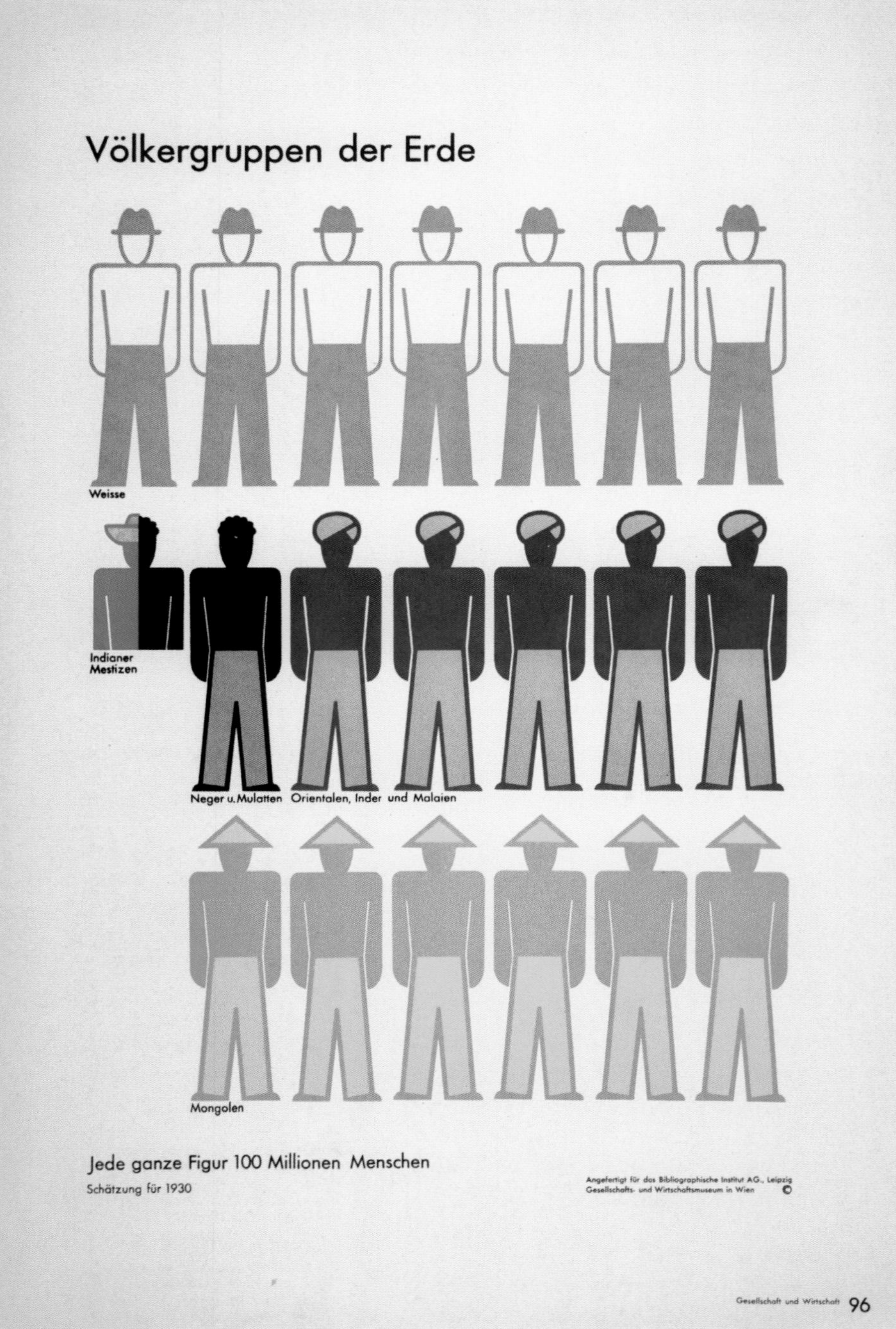
Völkergruppen der Erde
Weisse
Indianer
Mestizen
Neger u. Mulatten
Orientalen, Inder und Malaien
Mongolen
Jede ganze Figur 100 Millionen Menschen
Schätzung für 1930
Angefertigt für das Bibliographische Institut AG., Leipzig
Gesellschafts- und Wirtschaftsmuseum in Wien ©
Gesellschaft und Wirtschaft 96

133

UK rail franchises up for renewal

(Symbol = 5m journeys)

Route and current operator	Passenger journeys	Renewal	Shortlisted for new franchise
Intercity West Coast Virgin Trains	27m	Dec 2012	Stagecoach, FirstGroup, Keolis, Virgin Trains, Serco & Abellio
Greater Western First Great Western	84m	Mar 2013	FirstGroup
Essex Thameside c2c	32m	May 2013	National Express
Great Northern/Thameslink First Capital Connect	90m	Sep 2013	FirstGroup
Northern Northern Rail	84m	Sep 2013	Serco & Abellio
Intercity East Coast East Coast	18m	Dec 2013	Directly Operated Railways (Government owned)

Source: Deutsche Bank

134

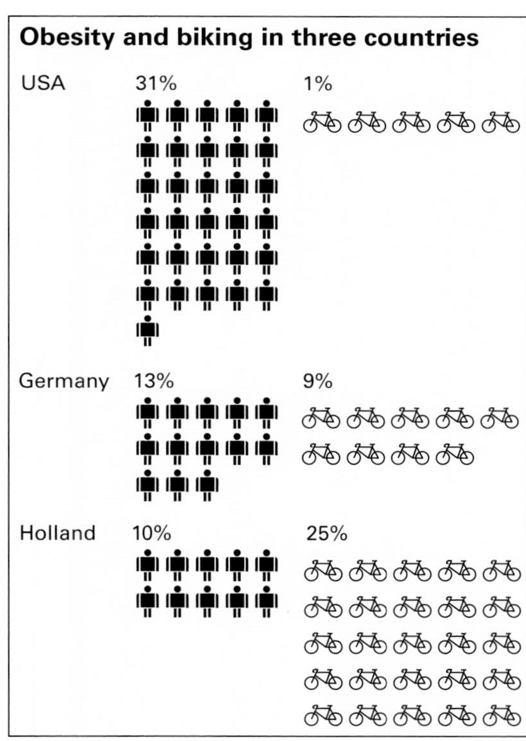

135

Figure 133 Völkergruppen der Erde, Population groups of the world.
Otto Neurath & Gerd Arntz
Gesellschaft und Wirtschaft, 1930.
Otto and Marie Neurath Isotype Collection, University of Reading

Figure 134 Each symbol on this scaled picture table stands for 5m journeys.
Data and design concept sourced from Financial Times, UK, 17 Jan 2012
From the Financial Times© The Financial Times Limited, 2012. All Rights Reserved

Figure 135 Obesity and biking. The picture table shows a strikingly negative correlation between obesity and biking in three nations.
Data sourced from: How Bikes Can Save US, Fast Company. www.fastcodesign.com/1665634/infographic-of-the-day-how-bikes-can-solve-our-biggest-problems

Heat maps

How do a large number of items compare?

A heat map is a table where the values are represented by colours instead of figures. Weak colours can indicate low (or normal) values while strong colours can indicate high (or outstanding) values. The merit of heat maps is that the viewer can spot interesting areas and patterns much faster than in a normal table. Heat maps are especially suited to describe financial markets. The Nasdaq and the S&P 500 heat maps exemplify this. Both are found on the Internet.

Heat maps can serve as surveillance systems for fast overview. Detailed information can be delivered backstage: for example, the Finviz website surveying S&P 500 allows readers to access details of specific securities using the mouseover function.

Figure 136 This display from the series *Five Years of Traffic Accidents* (in USA) exemplifies the strength of heat maps. The upper heat map relates traffic accidents to weekdays and hours. The lower heat map focuses on traffic accidents related to alcohol. Both heat maps also show numbers. The pattern around weekends is – while not surprising – alarming. Data and design sourced from: John Nelson, Fast Company, 2012. http://blog.fastcompany.com/post/38146002040/john-nelsons-infographic-five-years-of-traffic

	AM												PM											
	1	2	3	4	5	6	7	8	9	10	11	12	1	2	3	4	5	6	7	8	9	10	11	12
Su	1,997	2,201	2,530	1,825	1,224	867	801	628	582	658	733	899	1,116	1,200	1,012	1,425	1,472	1,468	1,605	1,550	1,452	1,307	1,163	930
M	725	650	705	484	442	643	936	979	604	733	860	926	1,061	1,161	1,227	1,368	1,335	1,409	1,324	1,161	1,181	1,081	902	809
T	625	575	561	399	349	646	911	916	629	756	829	855	946	1,097	1,210	1,388	1,365	1,332	1,268	1,199	1,135	1,115	829	827
W	769	660	624	466	452	642	888	945	622	722	783	878	957	1,046	1,160	1,366	1,296	1,272	1,351	1,180	1,186	1,264	1,023	928
T	823	767	807	523	434	704	915	936	721	759	827	917	942	1,020	1,185	1,300	1,364	1,375	1,331	1,258	1,258	1,247	1,173	1,053
F	1,040	1,010	1,056	712	543	762	936	975	775	739	931	1,065	1,096	1,261	1,406	1,583	1,516	1,627	1,639	1,522	1,522	1,774	1,865	1,916
Sa	1,705	2,075	2,460	1,515	1,184	933	893	774	794	870	987	1,146	1,290	1,200	1,452	1,513	1,502	1,664	1,737	1,700	1,712	1,759	1,714	1,875

	1	2	3	4	5	6	7	8	9	10	11	12	1	2	3	4	5	6	7	8	9	10	11	12
Su	67%	70%	76%	71%	69%	56%	45%	34%	25%	19%	13%	12%	11%	15%	18%	22%	27%	34%	40%	40%	44%	49%	51%	52%
M	62%	61%	65%	53%	36%	19%	12%	8%	6%	7%	8%	10%	3%	11%	12%	14%	17%	20%	26%	34%	39%	43%	46%	51%
T	59%	60%	61%	50%	33%	17%	10%	6%	9%	8%	6%	8%	9%	10%	12%	13%	15%	22%	24%	33%	37%	41%	44%	52%
W	59%	61%	64%	50%	37%	16%	11%	8%	6%	6%	9%	8%	11%	10%	13%	14%	16%	21%	25%	32%	37%	41%	49%	50%
T	62%	62%	72%	63%	42%	22%	14%	3%	9%	8%	10%	9%	3%	12%	13%	13%	16%	20%	25%	34%	40%	41%	49%	57%
F	64%	70%	71%	63%	46%	26%	17%	11%	11%	7%	8%	9%	10%	11%	14%	15%	20%	24%	29%	37%	41%	48%	50%	60%
Sa	66%	73%	76%	71%	56%	49%	36%	28%	16%	16%	10%	12%	12%	17%	21%	25%	30%	32%	39%	45%	49%	50%	55%	58%

136

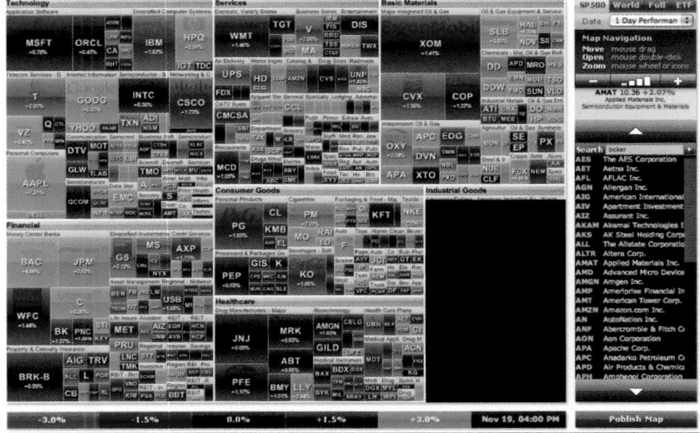

137A

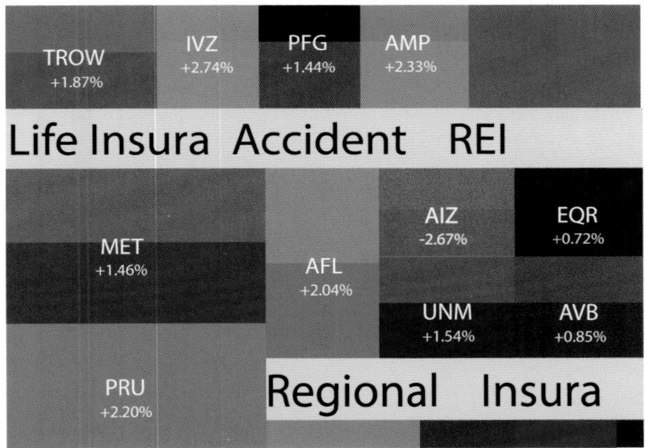

137B

Figure 137 S&P 500 heat map on the Finviz website shows the stocks of Standard & Poor's 500 top US companies. It is organised as a treemap *(see p149)* and stocks are represented by rectangles calibrated to show the importance of the stocks. Yellow rulers indicate the industry. Zoom functions allow viewers to go into detail. The detailed map (B) is redrawn from the website. Used with the permission of Finviz. www.finviz.com/map.ashx

Small multiples

What are the patterns?

Small multiples are also known as *Trellis charts*, *lattice charts*, *grid charts*, and *panel charts*.

One of the fundamental principles of data visualisation is to boil many figures down to one visual display that gives essential information by showing position, shape, size, and colour.

Sometimes, however, the parts of a whole warrant special interest. When this is the case, many smaller similar displays are better than one big display. A panel of smaller, similar displays may show patterns, tendencies, and irregularities that might otherwise remain hidden.

The displays of small multiples can be bar charts, bubble charts, line charts, maps, and many other types.

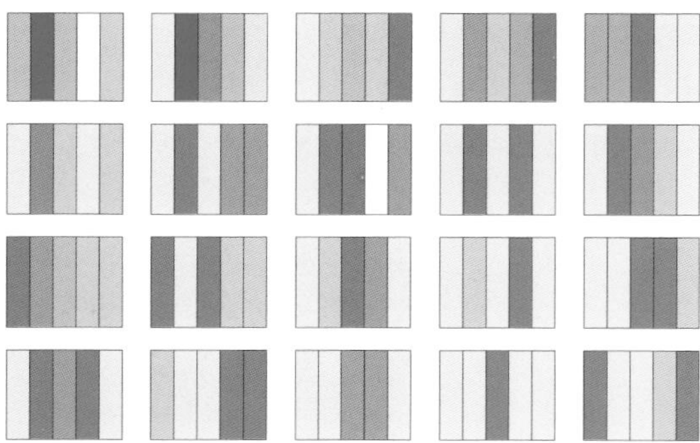

138

Figure 138 Multiple bars showing grades in a class. 20 students, five disciplines, five possible grades.

Figure 139 Multiple maps showing sales of a new product in Australian states.

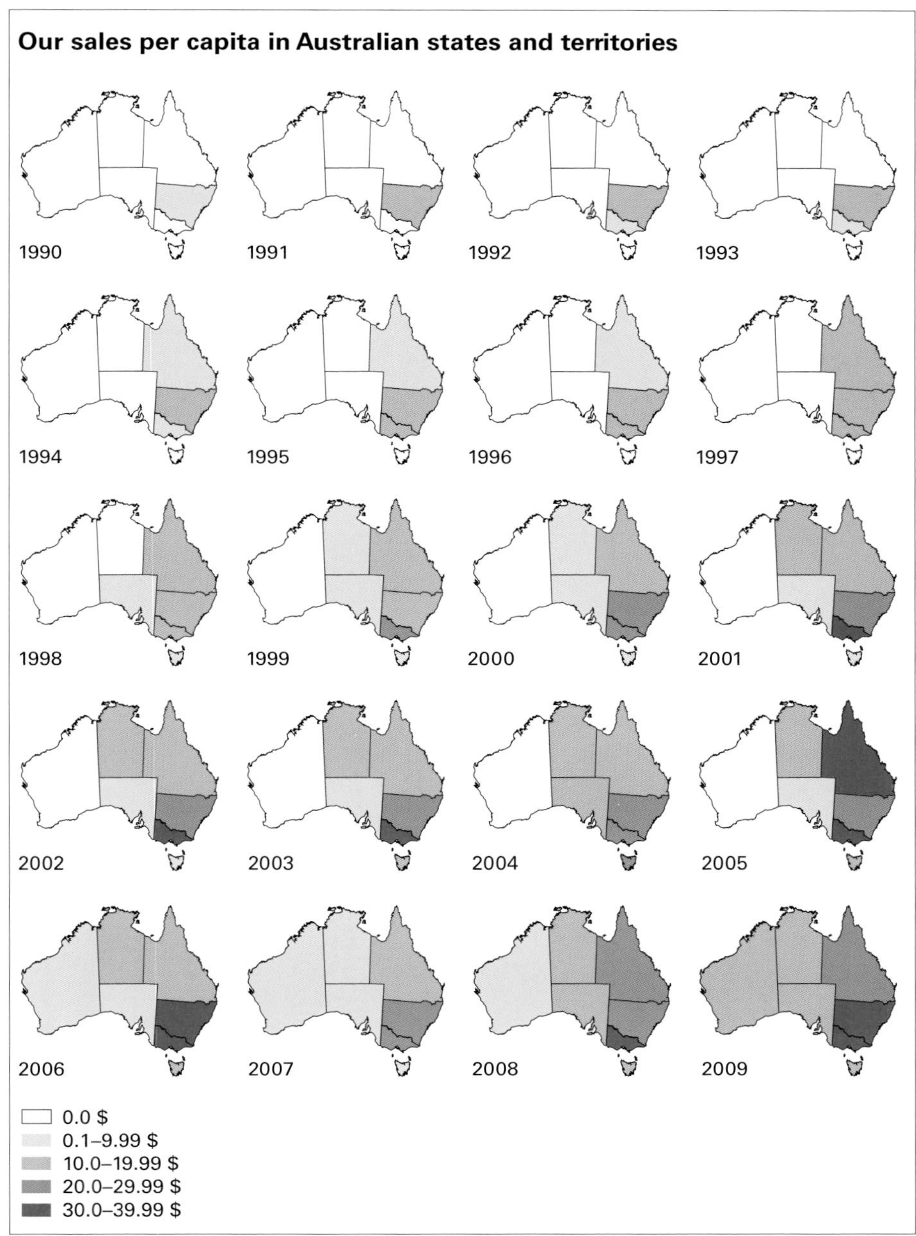
Our sales per capita in Australian states and territories
1990
1991
1992
1993
1994
1995
1996
1997
1998
1999
2000
2001
2002
2003
2004
2005
2006
2007
2008
2009
0.0 $
0.1–9.99 $
10.0–19.99 $
20.0–29.99 $
30.0–39.99 $

139

Don'ts

Simplicity is fundamental to good visual displays. Simple – but not overly simple – displays are easier to understand. First, their function is visible. What they are all about is not a riddle. They help readers to understand information rather than asking readers to solve a visual puzzle. Second, the information is easy to read. Simplicity is found on several levels.

Don't use more text than necessary. Don't drown your message in words. The great idea of data design is that your display should tell the story.

Don't use a larger type size than necessary. Necessary means big enough to let the intended audience read without problems.

Don't use more graphic effects than necessary. Readers want the message, not the wrapping.

Don't use more dimensions in your display than warranted by the content. One-dimensional values should in principle be shown in one dimension. To say 'in principle' means, for example, that the bars in bar charts should be thick enough to be noticed.

Use two-dimensional displays of one-dimensional variables with great care to let the readers know if they should read a length or an area. Don't use three-dimensional displays to show one-dimensional variables. The display does not become three times better, but it often becomes misleading.

In a perfect world, it would be easy to design good, simple, and engaging displays, and it would be difficult to design bad, unnecessary, complex, and complicated displays.
Our world is less than perfect. Modern computer software makes it easy to make displays that are difficult to understand and troublesome to read, as well as misleading. Some software makes bad displays natural.
Computer users with Microsoft Office are only a few clicks away from bar charts that lie by factors of seven or more.

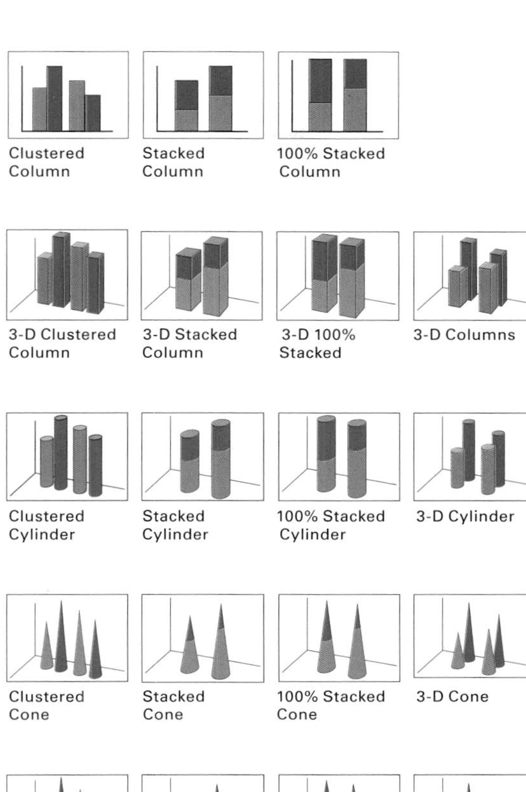

140

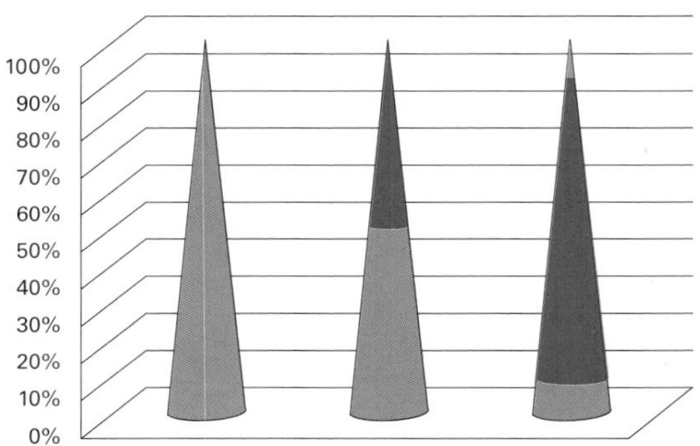

141

Figure 140 Microsoft Excel offers a large selection of chart types to choose from: vertical and horizontal bar charts, pie charts, donut charts, bubble charts, line charts, radar charts, and more. Each category includes several varieties, as does the vertical bar chart category as shown here – redrawn from Excel.
The top row shows ordinary 2-D bar charts; the next four rows show varieties of 3-D charts.
The three first of the four types in each row show what we in *Data Design* call *multiple bar charts*, *stacked bar charts*, and *divided-bar charts*. The 3-D charts are more difficult to read and understand correctly than the 2-D charts in the top row. The cones and pyramids in the two lowermost rows show incorrect and misleading volumes.

Figure 141 This cone display – redrawn from Excel – is extremely difficult to read. The total of each of the three cones should show 100%. The second cone should show a fifty-fifty distribution. However, the lower half is represented by a volume that is exactly seven times the volume representing the upper half.
The third cone should represent a 10/80/10% distribution. However the lower 10% is represented by 271 times the volume representing the upper 10%.

Don't show 1-D values in 3-D and never show them in cones or pyramids.

Visualising locations

Some of the visual displays in the previous chapter dealt with quantities relating to locations. Some, for example, compared population in Australian states and territories with vertical or horizontal bars used to represent different locations. The visual displays in this chapter show locations in a different way; they present the locations as dots, lines, and areas on thematic maps.

A short introduction to basic cartographic concepts will serve the designer of thematic maps as a useful mental foundation.

Visualising locations

Thematic maps

Geographic maps are flat, visual representations of smaller or larger parts of the surface of the Earth. Geographic maps are always designed for a purpose, and the quality of a map should be evaluated with this purpose in mind. Whatever the purpose, geographic maps are always selective and distortive. They highlight selected features of the represented world, while suppressing and excluding others.

This chapter is an introduction to the design of thematic maps, i.e. maps designed for special purposes.

General maps offer general topographic descriptions of areas and can be used for many purposes. Thematic maps show the existence of something particular related to geographic location, for example major industries, the average rainfall of different areas, or the trajectory of a new railway.

Thematic maps include two types of information: new information and supporting information.

New information

The new information addresses the purpose of the map directly. In the examples just mentioned, new information includes the major industries, the average rainfall, and the trajectory of the planned railway line.

Supporting information

Supporting information includes everything that assists understanding the new information. For example, this might be the borderline of a nation and the location of large cities. The known explains the unknown. What should be included in the supporting information depends on the specific purpose of the map and the presumed knowledge of prospective readers.

New information should stand out from supporting information to allow fast and precise reading. New information is the master, supporting information the servant.

Like other maps, thematic maps work with areas, lines, and points. Some thematic maps show the characteristics of a certain area: forest, rainfall, etc. Some thematic maps show lines such as railways. And, finally, some thematic maps show points, such as the locations of accidents.

Data Design is not a textbook on cartography and information designers working with thematic maps don't have to be professional cartographers. Designers should, however, have a basic knowledge of four cartographic concepts: map scale, map projection, the geographic coordinate system, and map orientation. The following four sections of *Data Design* present these concepts.

Map scale

For practical reasons, maps are smaller than the area they represent.* The ratio between a distance on the map and the corresponding distance in the real world is called *scale*. Terms such as *small-scale maps* and *large-scale maps* are not fixed, but 1:250,000 maps for motoring are typically called *small-scale maps* while 1:25,000 maps for walking are called *large-scale maps*. The scale of a map can be described in three ways: numerically, verbally, or graphically. On you-are-here maps, walking distance is occasionally shown in minutes.

*A full-scale map would, as Lewis Carroll observed, cover the fields making farmers unhappy.

Figure 142 Numerical, verbal, and graphic description of scale on British escape map of the Basra province in Iraq. Printed on silk.
War Office, 1942

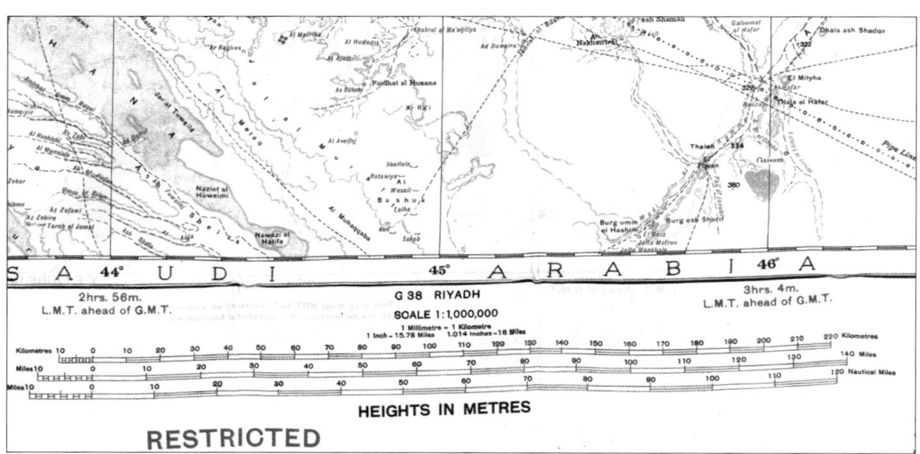

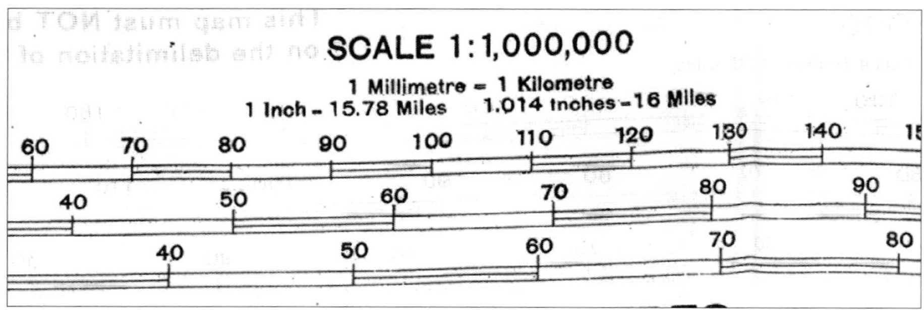

– *Numerical description of scale*
The ratio 1:100,000 (or the fraction 1/100,000) designates that 1 unit of distance on the map represents 100,000 units of distance in the real world. 1 centimetre on the map represents 100,000 centimetres (= 1 kilometre) in the real world. The units of the numerical description should always be the same in the numerator and the denominator (both sides of the colon). The larger the denominator (the number to the right of the colon) the smaller is the scale of the map. As the scale will change if the size of the map changes when copied, scanned, or placed on the web, careless reproduction may render the numerical description of scale inaccurate.

– *Verbal description of scale*
A verbal description of scale translates a numerical description into words: 'One centimetre on the map represents one kilometre in the real world.' This statement and similar statements will become incorrect if the size of the map is changed.

– *Graphic description of scale*
A graphic description of scale involves a line on the map that is said to correspond to a certain distance in reality. Graphic descriptions of scale will remain true if the size of the map is changed.

– *Walking time*
To pedestrians in cities, large airports, and similar environments estimated walking distance expressed in minutes may be more useful than exact distance in metres.

143

Figure 143 Walking time: understandable distance information in large pedestrian areas.

Map projection

Projection is the term for the method by which the curved surface of the Earth is transformed to be shown on a flat map. It always involves some kinds of distortion of areas, shapes, distances, or directions. While designers of the kinds of thematic maps in *Data Design* are not expected to make new projections, they should be aware of the projection-related problems inherent in maps of large areas.

The spherical – or rather almost spherical – shape of the Earth defies precise representation on a flat map. The Earth's surface is not developable; like the peel of an orange, it cannot be rolled out into a plane without distortion. In contrast to the sphere, cylinders and cones have developable surfaces. As a consequence, all planar maps of the Earth are projections, i.e. representations with some kind of distortion. For example, no planar map of the Earth can have a constant scale. The relevance of this imperfection increases with the size of the area represented by a map. Scale distortion is insignificant in a town map, but highly significant in a world map.

The projection of the surface of the Earth into a two-dimensional flat map can take place in several ways. Most world maps are created by first transposing the Earth's surface into a cylindrical surface (which is developable), and then rolling out the cylinder surface. This projection is known as *Mercator's Projection,* after the Flemish cartographer Gerardus Mercator (1512–1594) who introduced it in 1569.

Cylindrical projection exaggerates areas increasingly with distance from the equator. On most world maps, for example, Greenland appears more or less the same size as South America. In reality, South America is almost eight times bigger. In addition, the North Pole and the South Pole will be shown as horizontal lines with the same length as the equator, while they should only be points.

Other projections dispense with, or diminish the apparent weaknesses of Mercator's Projection, but no projection is correct in relation to areas, shapes, distances, and directions, all at the same time.

Figure 144 Mercator's Projection. Most world maps are created using the method developed by Flemish cartographer Gerardus Mercator in 1569. The world on Mercator's Projection between 82°S and 82°N. 15° graticule (latitude/longitude pattern). Imagery is a derivative of NASA's Blue Marble summer month composite. Image created with the Georcart map projection software.

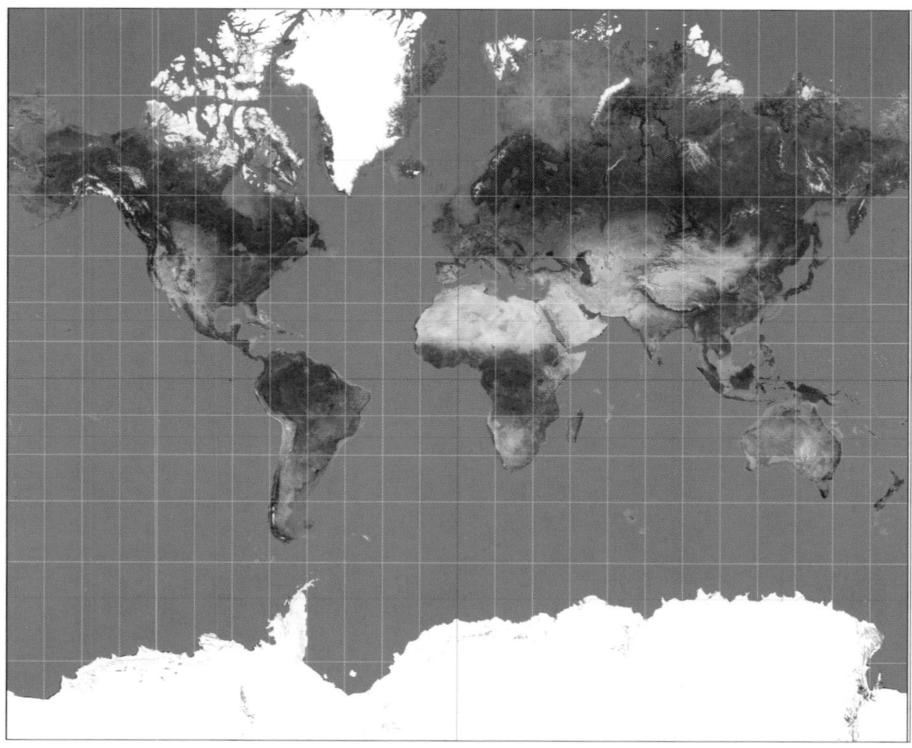

144

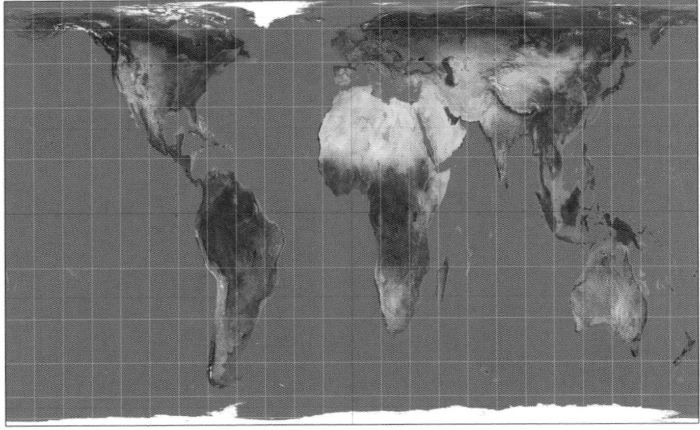

145

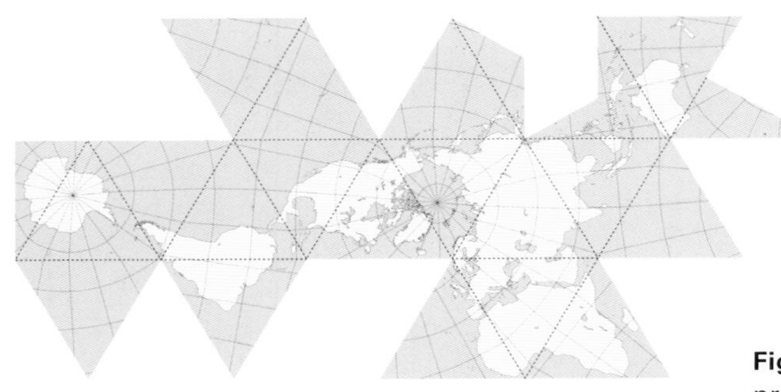

146

Figure 145 The Gall–Peters projection, invented by James Gall in 1863 and reintroduced by Arno Peters in 1973, has adjusted sizes of land areas.
A Gall–Peters projection of a Visible Earth image collected by the Earth Observatory experiment of the U.S. Government's NASA space agency.

Figure 146 Buckminster Fuller projected the Earth as an icosahedron: a polyhedron with twenty plane triangular faces; interesting, but not practical for most everyday purposes.
http://commons.wikimedia.org/wiki/File:Fuller_projection_rotated.svg
Author: Eric Gaba

Visualising locations

The geographic coordinate system

Positions on the Earth are referred to by latitude and longitude.

– *Latitudes*

Latitudes, also called *parallels*, run east to west. They describe the distance to the equator defined by the angle between the equator plane measured at its centre and a given position on the Earth's surface. Latitudes are indicated by 0–90° north or south relative to equator. All positions with the same latitude are positioned on a line parallel with the equator.

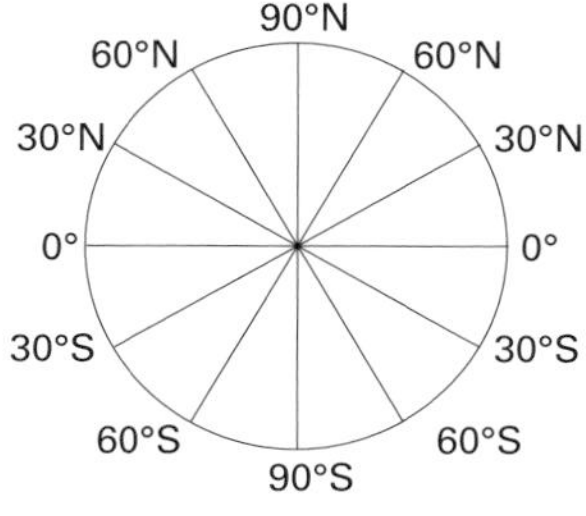

147

– *Longitudes*

Longitudes, also called *meridians*, run south to north. They describe the distance to the prime meridian, which by convention runs through the Greenwich Observatory in south-east London. Longitudes are indicated by 0–180° east or west relative to Greenwich. The distance between any pair of longitudes is largest at the equator and smallest (zero) at the North Pole and the South Pole.

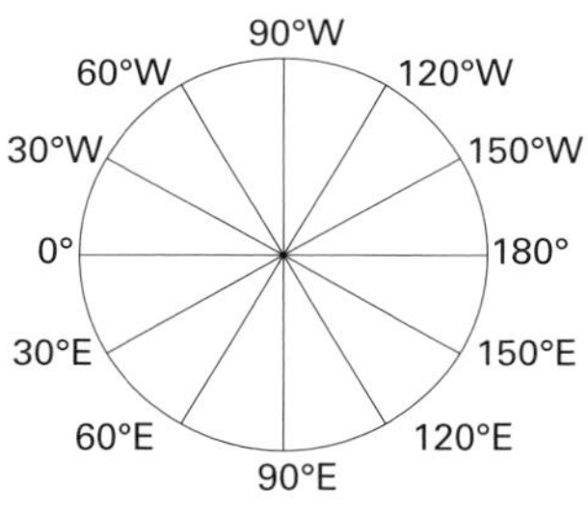

148

Selected geographic positions:

North Pole	90° N
Copenhagen	55.67° N, 12.57° E
Greenwich	51.48° N, 0°
New York	40.75° N, 74° E
Melbourne	37.81° S, 144.96° E
South Pole	90° S

Source: www.mygeoposition.com

Figure 147 Latitudes, also known as *parallels*.

Figure 148 Longitudes, also known as *meridians*.

Map orientation

Most maps are shown with north-up. This is a convention with no mathematical or geographic justification. The tradition is strong today, but this was not always so. The word *orientation* stems from the fact that old maps often have east (orient) up.

South-up roadmaps are occasionally delivered together with north-up maps to make map-reading easier for inexperienced map-readers when going south.

South-up maps are sometimes used for political reasons. On Australia Day in 1979, Stuart McArthur launched *McArthur's Universal Corrective Map of the World*.

As a rule, outdoor you-are-here maps have forward-up-alignment and north-up, but sometimes only forward-up-alignment or north-up *(see pp140/141)*.

149

Figure 149 South-up photo of the Earth. 'The Blue Marble' is the famous photograph of the Earth taken on December 7, 1972, by the crew of the Apollo 17 spacecraft en route to the Moon at a distance of about 29,000 kilometres (18,000 statute miles). It shows Africa, Antarctica, and the Arabian Peninsula.
When the crew of Apollo 17 took their famous photo, it showed the Earth with south-up. NASA, however, turned the photo upside down before releasing it.

Figure 150 There is nothing unnatural about it: a south-up map can just be impractical because of the strong tradition.

Figure 151 On maps of indoor areas – as a rule called *plans* – compass directions often have little or no meaning. Users tend to experience the place in a direction from the entrance and in.
ATC Advanced Technologies Centre, Swinburne University of Technology, Melbourne

Cyprus
(Turkey)
Greece
Turkey
Bulgaria
Serb.
Italy
Spain
Georgia
Romania
Hungary
Austria
Switz.
France
Czech Rep.
Ukraine
Poland
Germany
UK
Belarus
Lithuania
Latvia
Denmark
Russia
Sweden
Norway
Finland
Iceland
1 Slovakia
2 Moldavia
3 Portugal
4 Ireland
5 Albania
6 Montenegro
7 Kosovo
8 Macedonia
9 Estonia
10 Bosnia and Herzegovina
11 Croatia
12 Luxembourg
13 Netherlands
14 Belgium
15 Slovenia

150

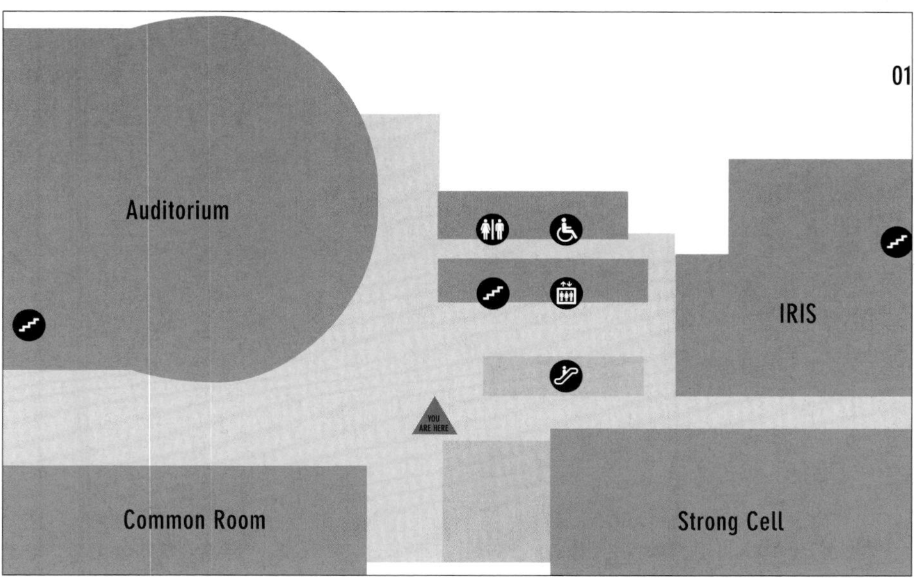
01
Auditorium
IRIS
YOU ARE HERE
Common Room
Strong Cell

151

Visualising locations

Choropleth maps

choro = area
pleth = multitude

How does an attribute vary with (predefined) geographic regions?

A choropleth map is a map where predefined regions are colour coded to show ranges or instances of a statistical variable. For example, such maps can represent rainfall, temperature, population density, or religion. The region is the independent variable while the attribute is the dependent variable. The colour codes must be explained in a legend. The virtue of choropleth maps is that they show location better than text alone would do.

The data of a choropleth map should be normalised, i.e. presented as an average, a rate, a density, or similar. Absolute magnitudes give inaccurate or mistaken impressions where areas of different size are involved. Viewers are tempted to weigh the measurement with the size of the area. Ranges of a quantitative variable should preferably be of equal size.

When the real-world variable is represented as a quantitative variable grouped in ranges, the colours should be used in a clearly rising order to enable overall reading without consulting the legend. If greytones or shades of a single hue, for example from light red to dark red, are used, readers should immediately get an idea how the highest values (represented by dark grey or dark or saturated red) are distributed.

If the attribute is a categorical variable, for example religion, a scale of different hues can be used. No specific order is needed, but clear difference is.

Figure 152 Choropleth map showing quantitative and qualitative data grouped in two sets of ranges, one for George Bush voters and one for John Kerry voters in the US 2004 presidential election. The colour progressions are not totally successful. In this respect, the colours representing Kerry voters are slightly better than the colours representing Bush voters. The ranges of the quantitative variable are of different size.

Figure 153 Choropleth map showing the US 2012 presidential election. Blue and red represent Obama / Democrats and Romney / Republicans respectively.

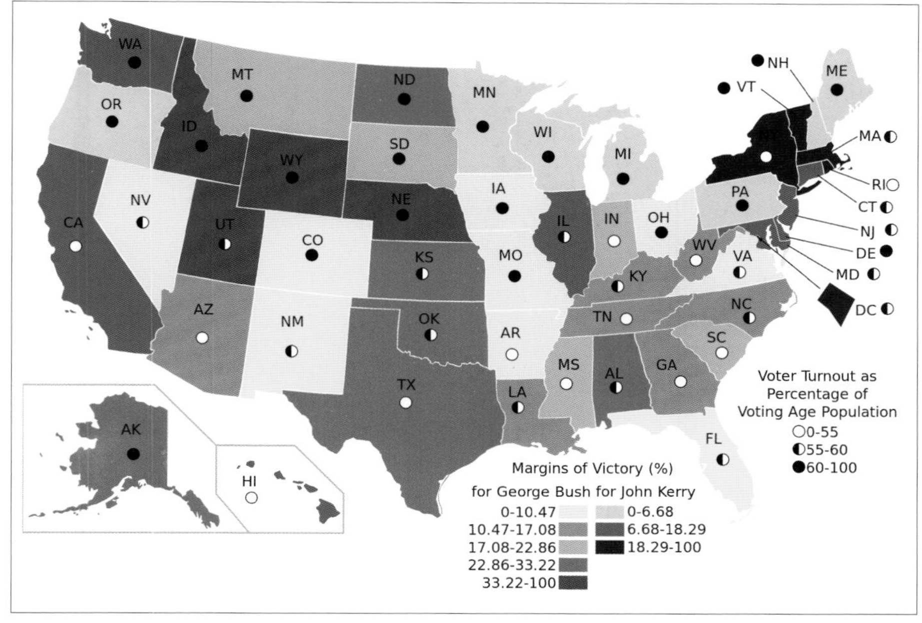
WA
OR
MT
ID
ND
MN
SD
WY
WI
MI
NH
VT
ME
MA
NV
CA
UT
CO
NE
IA
IL
IN
OH
PA
RI
CT
NJ
DE
MD
KS
MO
KY
WV
VA
AZ
NM
OK
TN
NC
DC
AR
SC
MS
AL
GA
TX
LA
AK
HI
FL
Voter Turnout as
Percentage of
Voting Age Population
0-55
55-60
60-100
Margins of Victory (%)
for George Bush for John Kerry
0-10.47
10.47-17.08
17.08-22.86
22.86-33.22
33.22-100
0-6.68
6.68-18.29
18.29-100

152

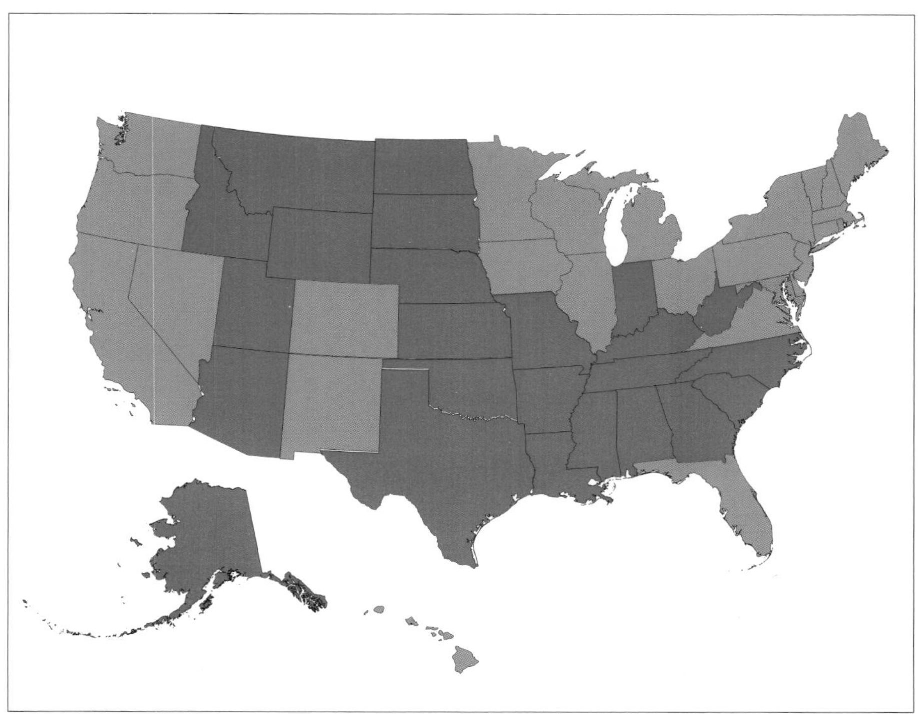

153

Proportional symbol maps

How much of a certain quality is where?

Proportional symbol maps show the presence of an attribute by symbols of proportional size. The location is the independent variable. The attribute is the dependent variable.

The most popular type of proportional symbol maps use dots as symbols. This is visible in maps that show cities with dots of different size according to the population.

The benefit of proportional symbol maps is that they give an immediate impression of the situation.

As the size of dots – or bubbles – and other two-dimensional symbols may be difficult to evaluate and compare, the symbols benefit from direct labels with amounts.

The symbols can be continuously variable or restricted to a limited number of ranges.

American cartographer James Flannery found that people tend to underestimate the size of dots (bubbles). They look at the diameter rather than the area. Consequently he suggested that chart designers use perceptual scaling instead of absolute (mathematically correct) scaling. Perceptual scaling implies that the size of dots grows more than by the absolute scaling.
We recommend that designers avoid this method.

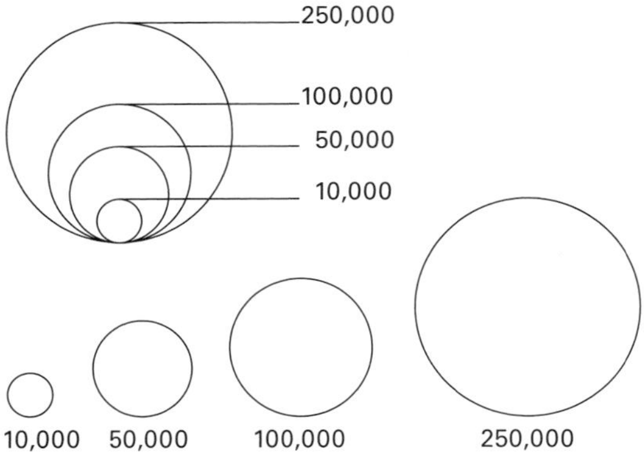

154

Figure 154 Examples of nested and linear legends for proportional symbol maps.

Figure 155 Proportional symbol map with dots.
Data sourced from http://www.water.gov.au

Figure 156 Proportional symbol map with vertical bar charts.
Data sourced from http://www.abs.gov.au

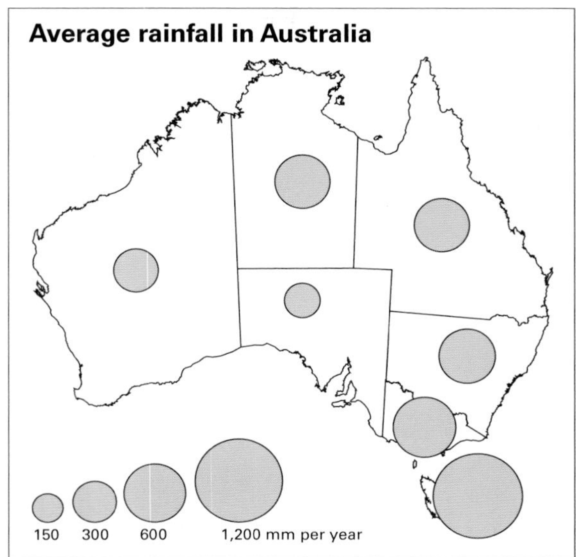
Average rainfall in Australia
150
300
600
1,200 mm per year

155

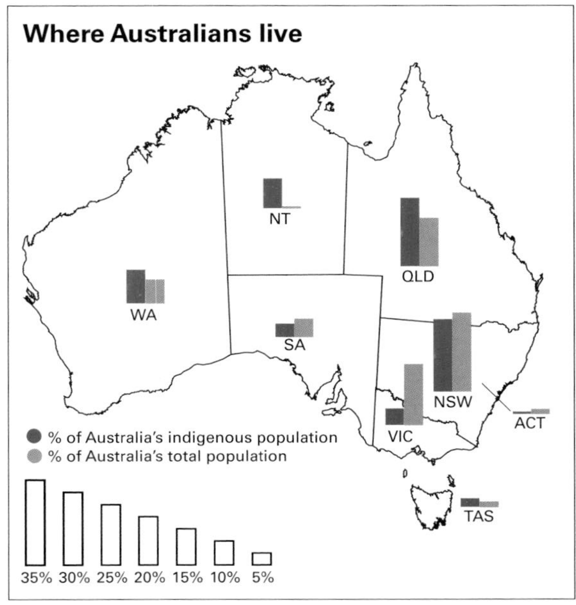
Where Australians live
NT
QLD
WA
SA
NSW
ACT
VIC
TAS
% of Australia's indigenous population
% of Australia's total population
35% 30% 25% 20% 15% 10% 5%

156

Isopleth maps

iso = same
pleth = multitude

How is a certain attribute distributed in a region?

Isopleth maps are also called *contour line maps*.

Whereas choropleth maps attach values to predefined areas, for example states or counties, isopleth maps create lines called *isopleths* with equal values of the statistical variable in question. Points in areas between two isopleths have values between the values of these.

Where a choropleth map shows, for example, average rainfall in predefined areas, an isopleth map shows lines with equal rainfall. In isopleth maps the attribute is the independent variable, while the location of the isopleths and the area between isopleths are dependent variables.

Isopleth maps are traditionally used to show altitude in land areas and depths in sea areas. Isopleth maps showing altitudes are also called *isohypses* and traditionally are connected with brownish colours. Isopleth maps showing water depths are also called *isobaths* and traditionally are connected with bluish colours.

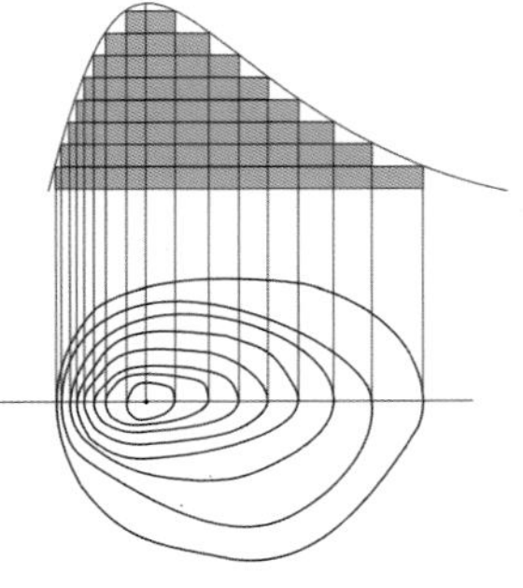

157

Figure 157 The principle of isopleth maps.
Creative Commons License – created by Romary, 2006

Figure 158 Simple isopleth map marking the Arctic region where the mean temperature in the warmest month (July) is below 10°C.
In public domain – United States Central Intelligence Agency's World Factbook

ARCTIC REGION
North Pacific Ocean
ALEUTIAN ISLANDS
Bering Sea
Petropavlovsk-Kamchatskiy
KURIL ISLANDS
occupied by the Soviet Union in 1945, administered by Russia, claimed by Japan.
JAPAN
Sakhalin
Sea of Okhotsk
Khabarovsk
Amur
Kodiak
Bethel
Gulf of Alaska
Anchorage
Valdez
Bering Strait
Nome
Provideniya
Anadyr'
Magadan
Okhotsk
Juneau
UNITED STATES
Fairbanks
Chukchi Sea
Arctic Circle
Pevek
Cherskiy
Oymyakon
Whitehorse
Dawson
Yukon
Wrangel Island
East Siberian Sea
Yakutsk
CHINA
Watson Lake
Prudhoe Bay
Barrow
average minimum extent of sea ice
Verkhoyansk
Mackenzie River
Inuvik
Beaufort Sea
Hay River
Echo Bay
Great Bear Lake
Yellowknife
Great Slave Lake
Lake Athabasca
NEW SIBERIAN ISLANDS
Tiksi
Lena
Banks Island
Laptev Sea
Victoria Island
Arctic Ocean
10°C (50°F) isotherm, July
Cambridge Bay
QUEEN ELIZABETH ISLANDS
CANADA
SEVERNAYA ZEMLYA
RUSSIA
Kangiqcliniq (Rankin Inlet)
Kaujuitoq (Resolute)
North Pole
90 W
90 E
Noril'sk
Yenisey
Hudson Bay
Repulse Bay
Ellesmere Island
Dikson
Kara Sea
Alert
Qaanaaq (Thule)
FRANZ JOSEF LAND
Baffin Island
Baffin Bay
Nord
Iqaluit (Frobisher Bay)
Longyearbyen
Svalbard (NORWAY)
NOVAYA ZEMLYA
Greenland (DENMARK)
Davis Strait
Barents Sea
Kangerlussuaq (Søndre Strømfjord)
Bjørnøya (NORWAY)
Greenland Sea
Nuuk (Godthåb)
Itseqqortoormiit (Scoresbysund)
Paamiut (Frederikshåb)
Tasiilaq (Ammassalik)
Jan Mayen (NORWAY)
Murmansk
Perm'
Tromsø
Arkhangel'sk
Labrador Sea
Narsarsuaq
Dvina
Denmark Strait
Norwegian Sea
Lake Onega
Kazan'
Samara
ICELAND
FINLAND
Reykjavík
NORWAY
Lake Ladoga
Nizhniy Novgorod
KAZ.
North Atlantic Ocean
Helsinki
St. Petersburg
Moscow
Saratov
SWEDEN
Tórshavn
Faroe Islands (DENMARK)
Tallinn
EST.
Oslo
Stockholm
Scale 1:39,000,000
Azimuthal Equal-Area Projection
SHETLAND ISLANDS
Riga
LATVIA
Volgograd
500 Kilometers
500 Miles
Vilnius
LITH.
Minsk
BELARUS
Baltic Sea
RUS.
Kharkiv
Rostov
Copenhagen
DENMARK
North Sea
Dnieper
The Arctic region is often defined as that area where the average temperature for the warmest month is below 10ºC.
Belfast
Warsaw
Kiev
UKRAINE
IRE.
Dublin
U.K.
Berlin
GERMANY
POLAND
Black Sea
802916AI (R02112) 6-02

158

Cartograms

How does a certain attribute vary with (predefined) geographic regions?

Cartograms are geographic maps distorted to show some geographically sensitive variable. There are two types of cartograms: area cartograms and distance cartograms.

Area cartograms distort the size of areas. Instead of showing the exact size of geographic surface, area cartograms adjust the size of regions to represent amounts of population, production, a natural resource, or another attribute. The region is the independent variable, the attribute shown as the new size of the region is the dependent variable.

Area cartograms are also known as *anamorphic maps*, *value-by-area maps*, and *density-equalising maps*.

In non-contiguous cartograms regions keep their shape but are adjusted in size and not connected. In contiguous cartograms the regions are adjusted in size and in form to be connected.

There is no fixed method to make contiguous cartograms, infinite solutions are possible, but the designer will try to make the map as recognisable as possible.

Two special types of area cartograms are *Dorling cartograms* and *Demers cartograms*, which replace all area shapes with calibrated circles and squares, respectively.

Figure 159 Distance cartogram showing distances from Heathrow Airport, Terminals 1, 2, and 3 in minutes by the Tube. The cartogram is part of a dynamic web application with mouseover details.
Design: Tom Carden, 2006
http://www.tom-carden.co.uk/p5/tube_map_travel_times/applet/

Proportional symbol maps are a good alternative to area cartograms. Where area cartograms use area size as a visual variable to show magnitude, proportional symbol maps use dots or other symbols and keep area sizes – and shapes – unchanged. Proportional symbol maps are easier to work with, both for sender and receiver, for designer and reader.

Distance cartograms distort distances. Instead of showing distances in kilometres, distance cartograms show distances measured by transport time, freight rates, or another attribute related to distance. The route is the independent variable, the (new) 'distance' is the dependent variable.

Distance cartograms are also called *central-point cartograms*.

159

160A

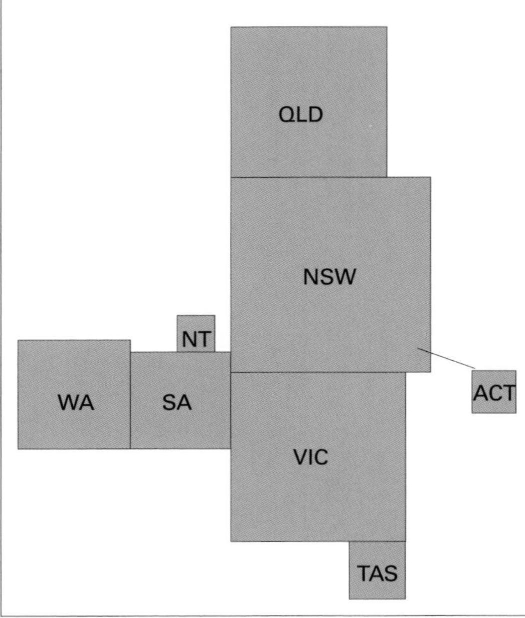

160B

Figure 160 Australia reconfigured in non-contiguous cartogram (A) and Demers cartogram (B) to represent population in states and territories:
New South Wales 7.25m
Victoria 5.57m
Queensland 4.51m
Western Australia 2.37m
South Australia 1.85m
Tasmania 0.51m
Aust. Capital Territory 0.37m
Northern Territory 0.23m.

Figure 161 Dynamic Dorling cartograms showing the development of obesity in USA 1995–2008.
Independent variables are geographic location and year. Dependent variables are obesity in absolute amounts shown by the size of the bubbles, and in percentage shown by the colour of the bubbles.
In 2008 there were most obese people in California, but it is a big state and the problem is largest in Missouri and Alabama.
The bipolar progression between greenish and reddish shades (green = good, red = bad) works fine, at least for readers not suffering from colour blindness.
Note that North Carolina is located south of South Carolina, for space reasons perhaps?
Design concept sourced from http://hci.stanford.edu/jheer/files/zoo/ex/maps/cartogram.html
Stanford HCI Group based on data from National Center for Chronic Disease Prevention and Health Promotion.

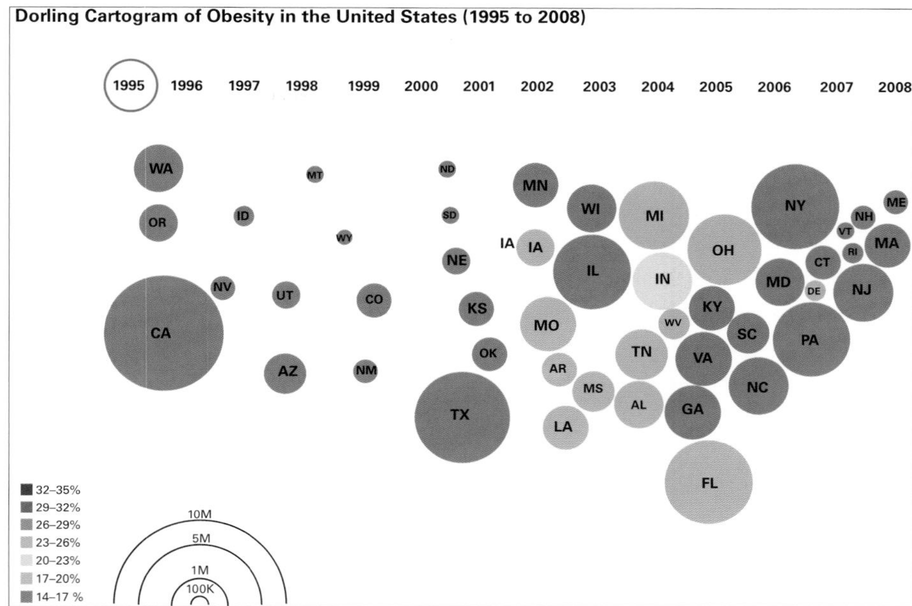
Dorling Cartogram of Obesity in the United States (1995 to 2008)
1995 1996 1997 1998 1999 2000 2001 2002 2003 2004 2005 2006 2007 2008
WA
OR
CA
NV
ID
UT
AZ
MT
WY
CO
NM
ND
SD
NE
KS
OK
TX
MN
IA
MO
AR
LA
WI
IL
MI
IN
MS
TN
AL
KY
WV
OH
VA
GA
FL
SC
NC
NY
PA
MD
DE
NJ
CT
RI
MA
VT
NH
ME
32–35%
29–32%
26–29%
23–26%
20–23%
17–20%
14–17 %
10M
5M
1M
100K

161A

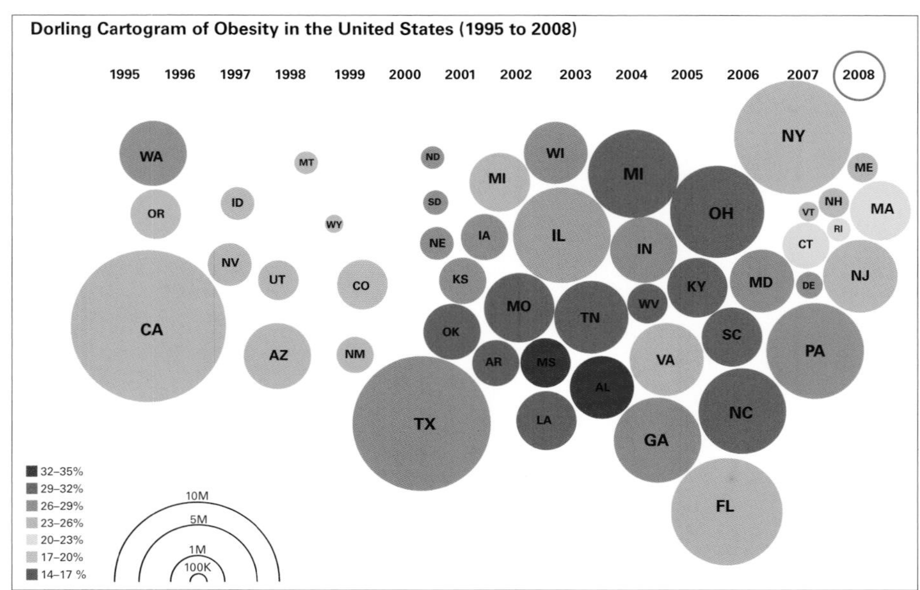
Dorling Cartogram of Obesity in the United States (1995 to 2008)
1995 1996 1997 1998 1999 2000 2001 2002 2003 2004 2005 2006 2007 2008
WA
OR
CA
NV
ID
UT
AZ
MT
WY
CO
NM
ND
SD
NE
KS
OK
TX
IA
MI
WI
IL
MO
AR
MS
LA
TN
AL
MI
IN
WV
OH
KY
VA
GA
FL
SC
NC
MD
NY
ME
VT
NH
MA
RI
CT
DE
NJ
PA
32–35%
29–32%
26–29%
23–26%
20–23%
17–20%
14–17 %
10M
5M
1M
100K

161B

Chorochromatic maps

choro = area
chromatic = coloured

How is a certain attribute distributed?

Chorochromatic maps define areas with specific qualities such as soil, vegetation, industrial use, or other attributes. The attribute is the independent variable while the area is the dependent variable. The independent variable is categorical. The dependent variable is quantitative.

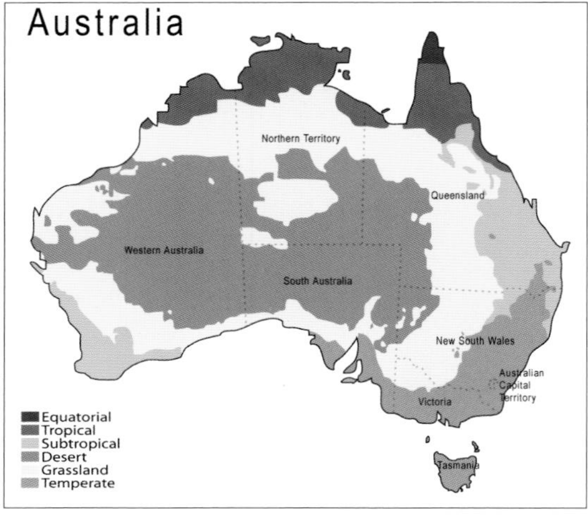

162

Figure 162 Chorochromatic map showing climatic zones in Australia.
Based on a modified Köppen classification system. Classification derived from 0.025 x 0.025 degree resolution mean rainfall, mean maximum temperature, and mean minimum temperature gridded data. All means are based on a standard 30-year climatology (1961 to 1990). From the Bureau of Meteorology.
The information is from the source of the original image: http://www.bom.gov.au/iwk/climate_zones/map_1.shtml

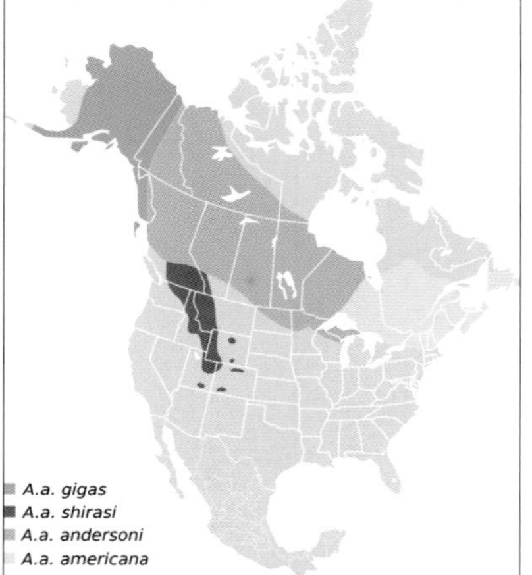

163

Figure 163 Chorochromatic map showing distribution of the North American subspecies of the moose, Alces alces, in North America.
Feldhammer, George A., Bruce C. Thompson, and Joseph A. Chapman, eds. Wild Mammals of North America: Biology, Management, and Conservation. pg 931. fig 4.1. ©1982, 2003.
Reprinted with the permission of John Hopkins University Press

Visualising locations
Dot distribution maps

Where does a certain thing happen?

There are more people who design and use dot distribution maps than those who know the name. A dot distribution map is what any road authority designs when they want to see where serious traffic accidents happen. They take an existing map and place dots where appropriate to represent accidents.

The most famous historical example of a dot distribution map was developed during the 1854 cholera outbreak in London when Dr John Snow designed a simple street map with dots where people had died from cholera. Public water pumps were also marked on the map. This led Dr Snow directly to one dangerous source, the public water pump on the corner of Broad Street and Cambridge Street. Removing the pump handle was followed by an immediate decrease in the number of cholera cases in the area.

Dr Snow's dot distribution map also settled the debate between those who thought that the source of cholera was infected air and those who thought that contaminated water or food was the source.

Figure 164 Dr Snow's dot distribution map showing locations of cholera cases and public water pumps, London, 1854.
Source: en.wikipedia.org/wiki/File:Snow-cholera-map-1.jpg

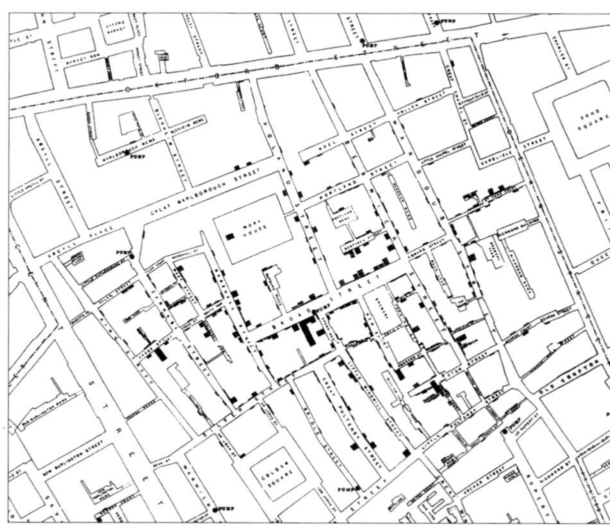

164

Transit maps

How do we get from station A to station B?

Transit maps are diagrams that represent the lines of a transportation system such as a metro. Transit maps concentrate on the sequence of stations and the connections between them, thereby allowing passengers to understand the system. To do this, they abstract from several geographic realities. Transit maps are topologic rather than topographic. They abstract from physical distance and location but have the relations between stations correct.

Transit maps are also known as *diagrams* and *schematics*.

The most famous, but not the first, transit map is the Tube map designed by Henry Charles Beck (nicknamed *Harry Beck*) for London Underground in 1931 *(see p38)*. Since then, the Tube map has been changed many times, but it remains basically the same.

The principles used in the Tube map and most other transit maps are these:

- Only give the necessary information. In the Tube map, the river Thames is the only supporting information.

- Only use horizontal and vertical lines plus diagonal lines of 45 degrees.

- Equalise visual distances between stations by exaggeration and reduction. This means that distances between stations near the centre are exaggerated to improve readability, while distances between stations away from the centre are reduced to limit the size of the map.

Figure 165 Paris Metro map.
Source: RAPT

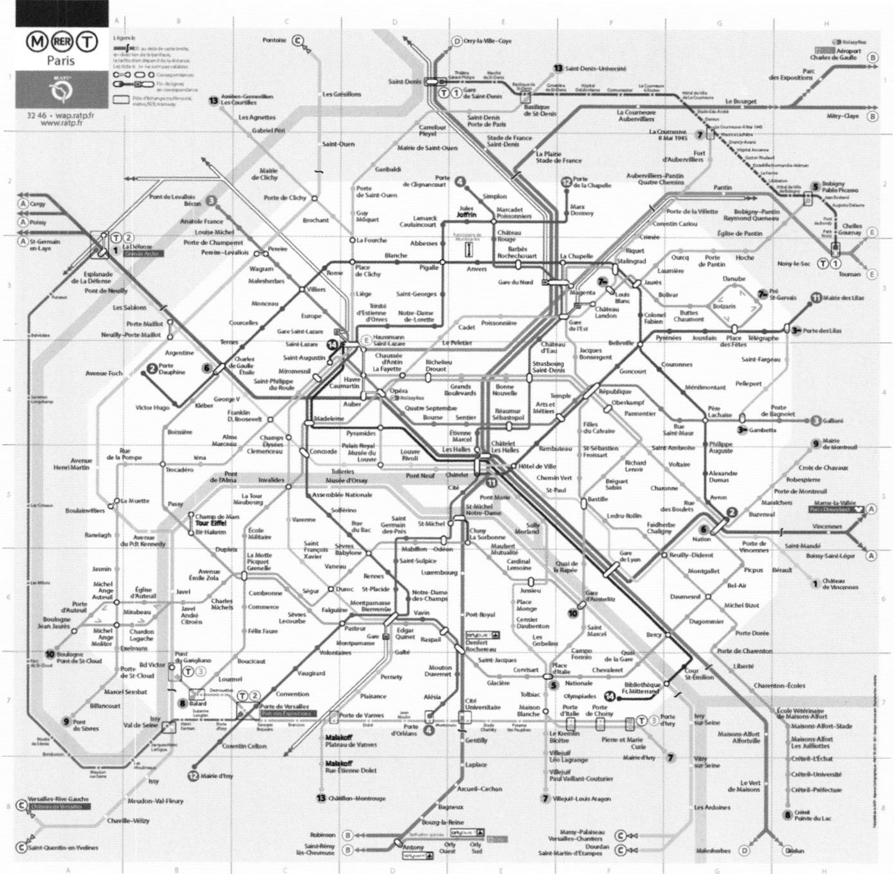

165

You-are-here maps

Where am I?
How can I reach what from here?

You-are-here maps, also called *y-a-h maps*, are maps shown at the entrance or in the middle of somewhere with a dot or arrow indicating the position of the map and the reader.

In order to function optimally, y-a-h maps must have forward-up-alignment. What is up on the map is forward in the terrain.

Also, the y-a-h map should in many situations preferably have a north-up orientation, because that is the way some users will already know the area from other maps.

The combination of forward-up-alignment and north-up orientation implies that the y-a-h map must face south if it is shown vertically, free-standing or mounted on a wall.

As with other large-scale maps used for wayfinding, the correspondence between map and terrain is of paramount importance. Comparing the map and the reality should enable clear recognition.

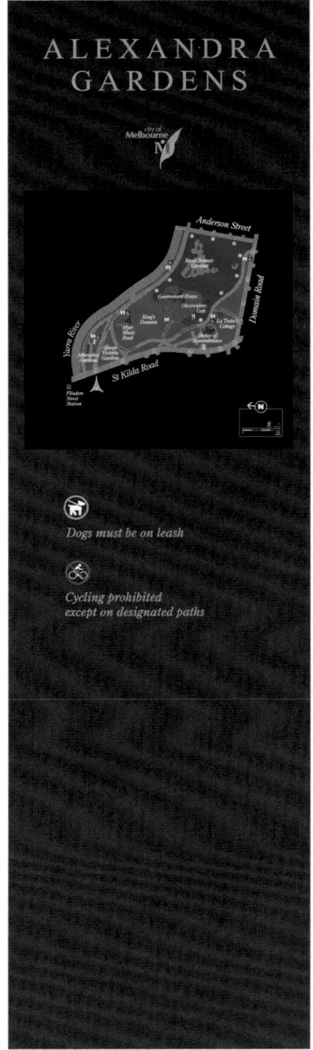

166A

Figure 166 Boot-shaped y-a-h map for walk along the Yarra River, Melbourne. The map has forward-up-alignment. North is to the left. The scale is indicated graphically and by walking time (lower right corner). Design: Letterbox

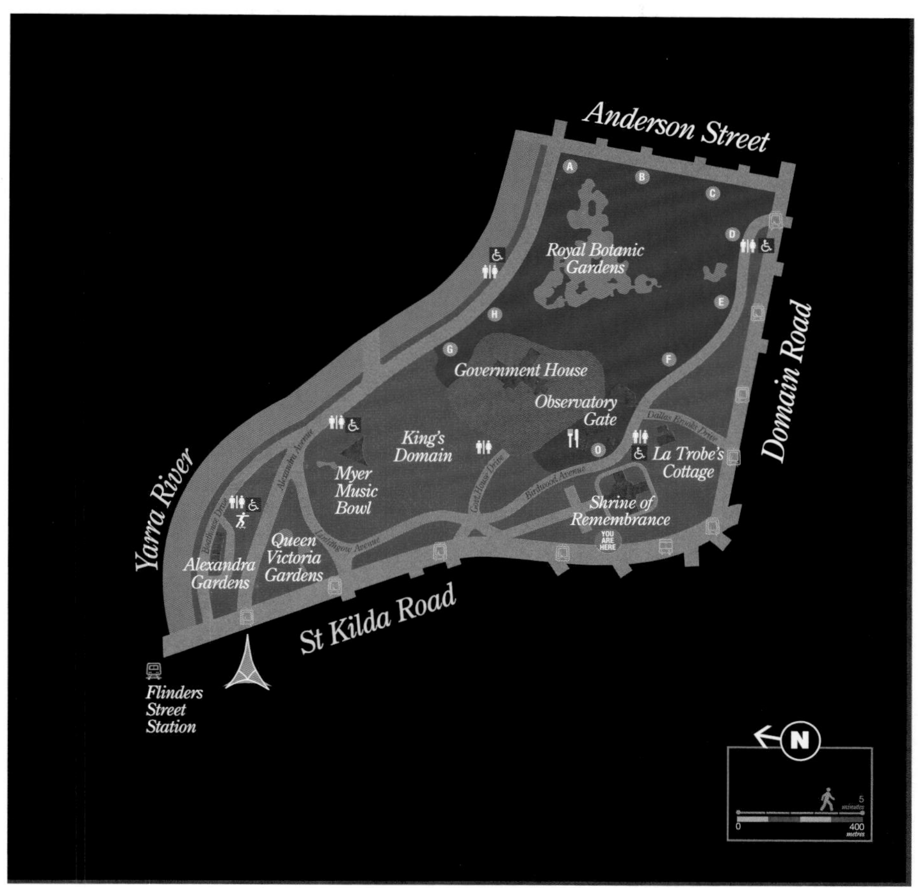
Anderson Street
Royal Botanic Gardens
Government House
Observatory Gate
King's Domain
Myer Music Bowl
La Trobe's Cottage
Shrine of Remembrance
YOU ARE HERE
Queen Victoria Gardens
Alexandra Gardens
Yarra River
Domain Road
St Kilda Road
Flinders Street Station
N
5 minutes
0
400 metres

166B

Visualising connections

We live in a complex world, which will probably not become less complex in the future. Few are likely to contest this. Complexity implies numerous interrelated elements, and ways that elements interrelate is the subject of the visual displays in this chapter.

The urge and the ability to express simple relations visually seem to be universal. We don't take classes to draw arrows, nested circles, pyramids, and stairs to show that something comes before, controls, or contains something else. The displays discussed in this chapter go a step further.

Trees

How is the hierarchy of a complex system?

A tree is a hierarchical data structure with a number of nodes that branches out from a single root node. The root node has no parent – immediately superordinate connection.
All other nodes have one, and only one, parent. Any node can have any number of children – immediately subordinate connections.
A node can only be directly connected with its parent and children. This rule precludes cycles.

The tree structure is found in all parts of life, in nature, and in the human-made world. Tree displays are used to visualise many kinds of classifications, contents, and organisational structures.

When used for classification, the tree structure implies that we look for similarities when we move from one node to another in the direction of the root, and for differences when we move away from the root.

A semantic weakness of the tree metaphor is that we normally show the visual tree display upside down with the root node at the top and the subordinated nodes below.
Available space sometimes dictates that we use a horizontal tree with the root to the left branching out to the right.
Some visual tree displays are so flat in structure – the root node has several immediately subordinate nodes – that these trees should rather be called *shrubs*.

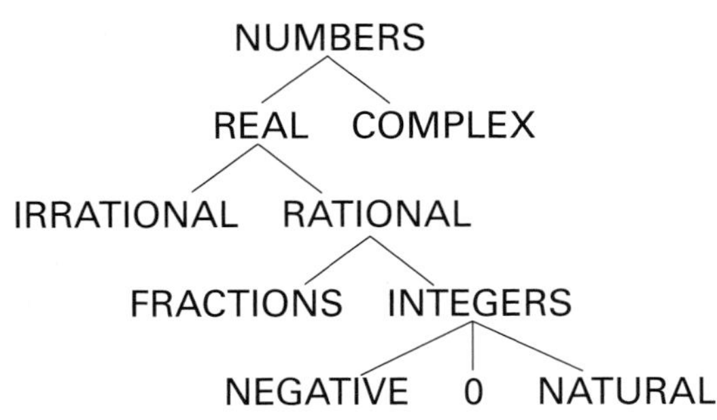

167

Figure 167 Tree codifying numbers.

Figure 168 Organogram used for showing command structure.

Figure 169 Sometimes only part of a tree is interesting, e.g. the family dog's family.

Figure 170 Ascending family tree.

Figure 171 Descending family tree.

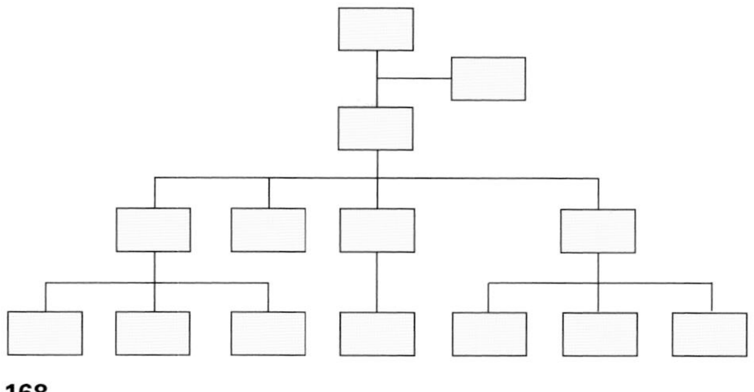

168

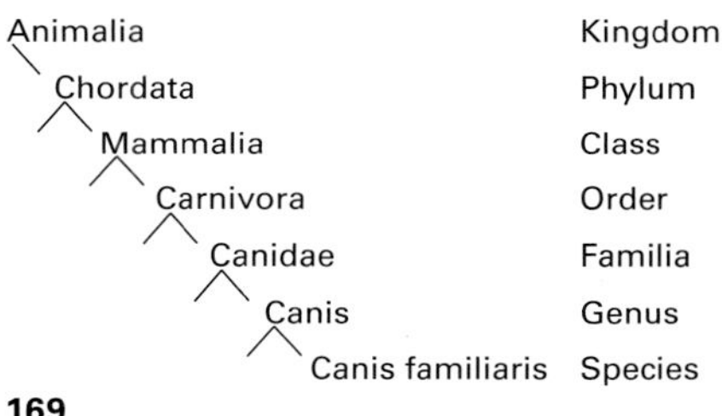

169

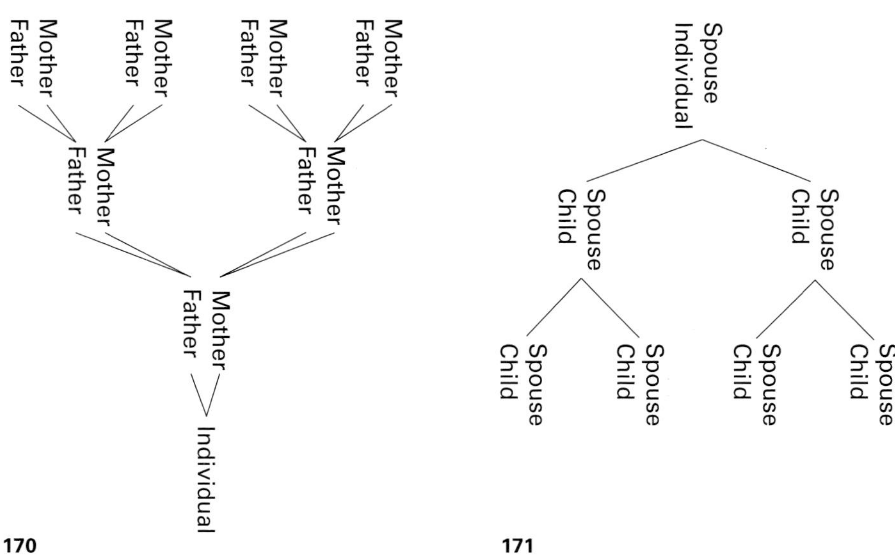

170

171

Trademarks	Graphic marks	Picture marks	Figurative marks	*Descriptive marks*	
				Metaphoric marks	
				Found marks	
			Non-figurative marks		
		Letter marks	Name marks	*Proper names*	
				Descriptive names	
				Metaphoric names	
				Found names	
				Artificial names	
			Abbreviations	Initial abbreviations	*Acronyms*
					Non-acronym initial abbreviations
				Non-initial abbreviations	
	Non-graphic marks				

172

Simplicity	Background	Home of simplicity	
	Fields of simplicity		
	Definition	Complex	
		Complicated	
	Parameters	Number of parts	
		Variety	
		Structure	
	Motives	Functionality	
		Aesthetics	Minimalism
			Exit ornament
		Ethics	The Shakers
	Forced simplicity		
	A modern choice		
	Occam's razor		
	Einstein's warning		

173

Figure 172 Horizontal tree showing a complete taxonomy of trademarks. Per Mollerup, *Marks of Excellence: The history and taxonomy of trademarks,* 1997, 2013

Figure 173 Tree structure used in the author's keynote presentation at Design Research Society's Wonderground conference, Lisbon, 2008

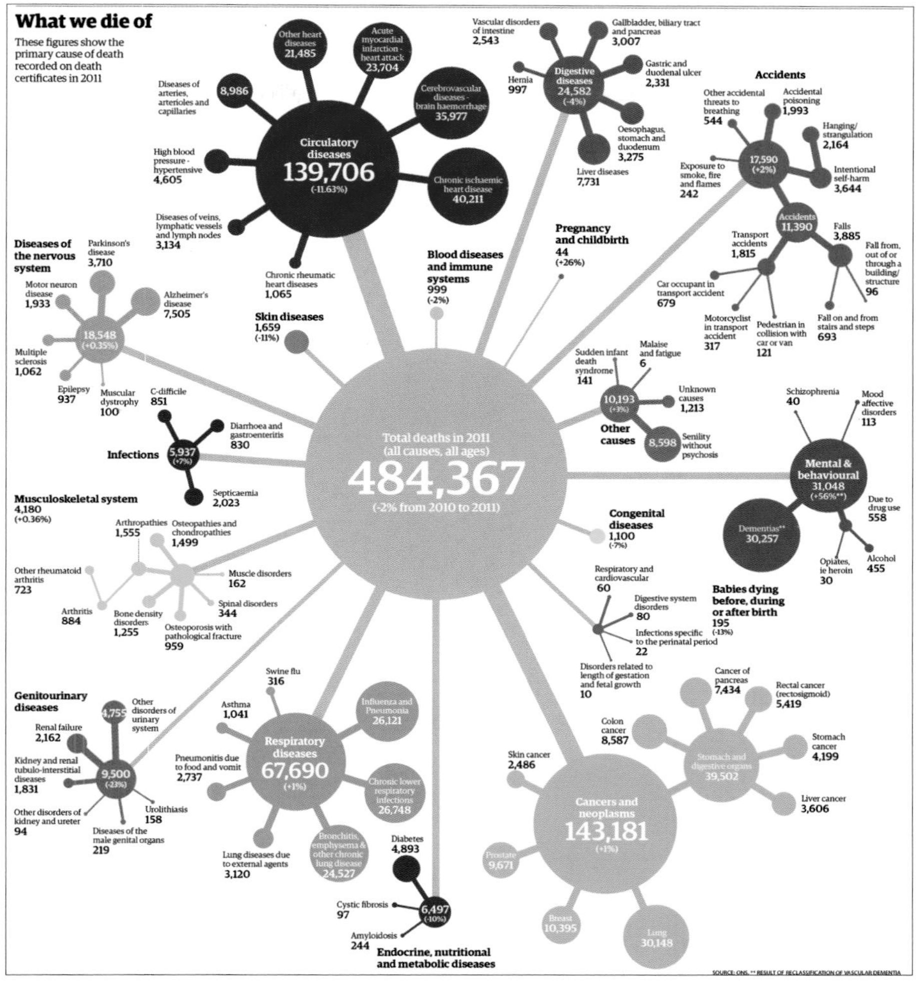

174

Figure 174 Tree structures with many branches often take circular forms. This tree of mortality causes is both a tree and a bubble chart. The size of the bubbles quantifies the causes, the colours group them. Copyright Guardian News & Media Ltd 2012

Decision trees

How should we weigh economic factors when taking a decision?

A decision tree represents the options from which a choice must be made. A tree structure organises the options with expected costs and possible outcomes and their probabilities in a way that allows a rigorous analysis and an informed decision.

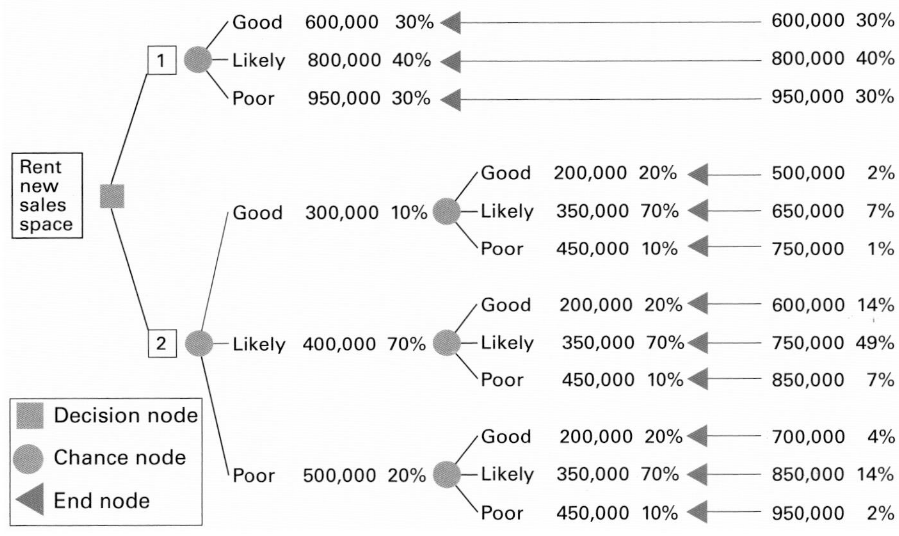

175

Figure 175 Decision tree describing a situation where a company looking for new sales space has two options: to rent space ready for use (1), or to look for space that needs some adaption (2). The option with the lowest expected costs is found by adding the possible costs multiplied with their probability:
785,000 for option 1.
740,000 for option 2.

Visualising connections

Treemaps

What is the hierarchy of a complex system?

Treemaps are visual hierarchies invented by Ben Shneiderman in the early 1990s. Nodes are pictured as nested rectangles dimensioned according to the value of the node.

The rectangles can be colour coded to reveal patterns which otherwise may be difficult to recognise. If a treemap is used to show support of political parties in a large number of geographical units, the amount of a specific colour will reveal one party's support.

Like pie charts and divided-bar charts, treemaps show parts of a whole, but do so in a way that allows organised presentation of a large number of parts. Treemaps are economical with space.

Treemaps can have one or more layers. One-layer maps have all information immediately visible. On-screen multi-layer treemaps allow the viewer to activate rectangles to see new subdivisions.

The values represented in a treemap are easiest to compare if the rectangles are squarish. At the same time the treemap should preferably be organised in a systematic manner. These two demands tend to conflict, good squarish fields tend to give messy charts, while good organisation tends to give some slim rectangles.

176

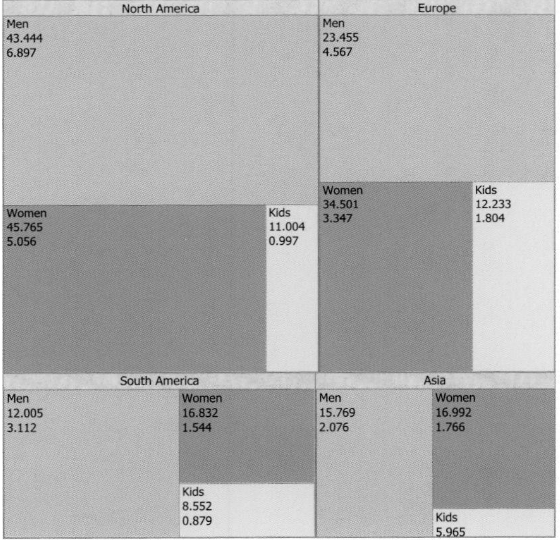

177

Figure 176–178 Treemaps visualising sales and profit of a clothing company. Geographical area and product category are independent variables. Sales and profit are dependent variables.

Figure 176 Treemap organised after area and product category. Product category is shown by colour, and sales is shown by size.

Figure 177 Treemap organised after area and product category. Product category is shown by colour, and profit is shown by size.

Figure 178 Treemap organised after product category and area. Sales are shown by colour, and profit is shown by size.

Figure 179 Web-based news site. The tabs at the bottom define the colour codes of the various subject areas. www.newsmap.jp

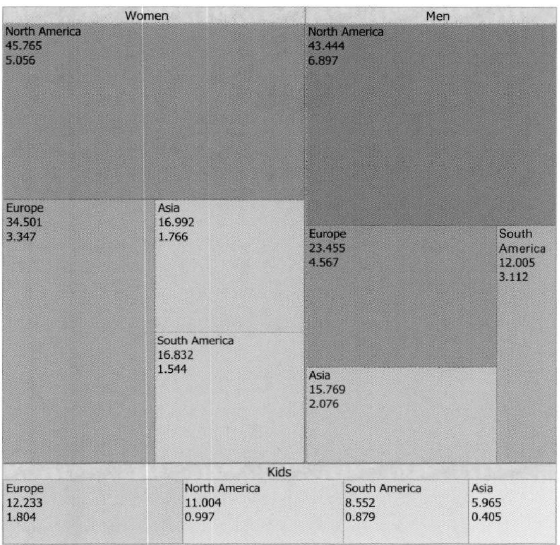
Women
North America
45.765
5.056
Europe
34.501
3.347
Asia
16.992
1.766
South America
16.832
1.544
Men
North America
43.444
6.897
Europe
23.455
4.567
South America
12.005
3.112
Asia
15.769
2.076
Kids
Europe
12.233
1.804
North America
11.004
0.997
South America
8.552
0.879
Asia
5.965
0.405

178

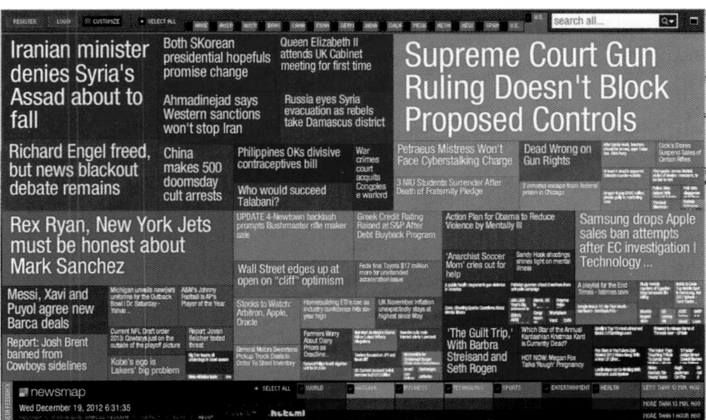
Iranian minister denies Syria's Assad about to fall
Both SKorean presidential hopefuls promise change
Queen Elizabeth II attends UK Cabinet meeting for first time
Ahmadinejad says Western sanctions won't stop Iran
Russia eyes Syria evacuation as rebels take Damascus district
Supreme Court Gun Ruling Doesn't Block Proposed Controls
Richard Engel freed, but news blackout debate remains
China makes 500 doomsday cult arrests
Philippines OKs divisive contraceptives bill
Who would succeed Talabani?
Petraeus Mistress Won't Face Cyberstalking Charge
Dead Wrong on Gun Rights
Rex Ryan, New York Jets must be honest about Mark Sanchez
Wall Street edges up at open on "cliff" optimism
Samsung drops Apple sales ban attempts after EC investigation | Technology ...
Messi, Xavi and Puyol agree new Barca deals
Report: Josh Brent banned from Cowboys sidelines
'The Guilt Trip,' With Barbra Streisand and Seth Rogen
search all...
newsmap
Wed December 19, 2012 6:31:35

179

Mind maps

How do several ideas, concepts, or phenomena relate to each other?

Mind maps are also known as *spidergrams* and *spidergraphs*.

Mind maps are displays developed around a central word or concept. Mind maps can be used for taking notes and developing, studying, and communicating ideas. Mind maps have tree structures. That might not be immediately clear because of their circular form.

Tony Buzan, who claims to have developed the modern mind map, presents ten guidelines for working with mind maps in *The Mind Map Book (see figure 180).*

Figure 180 Tony Buzan presents his ten guidelines in this mind map. *Data Design* suggests a more restricted use of effects. Mind Map is a registered trademark of the Buzan Organisation Limited 1990, www.thinkbuzan.com. Creative Commons License – created by Nicoguaro, 2011

Figure 181 Mind map used as lecture cues. Courtesy of Ken Friedman

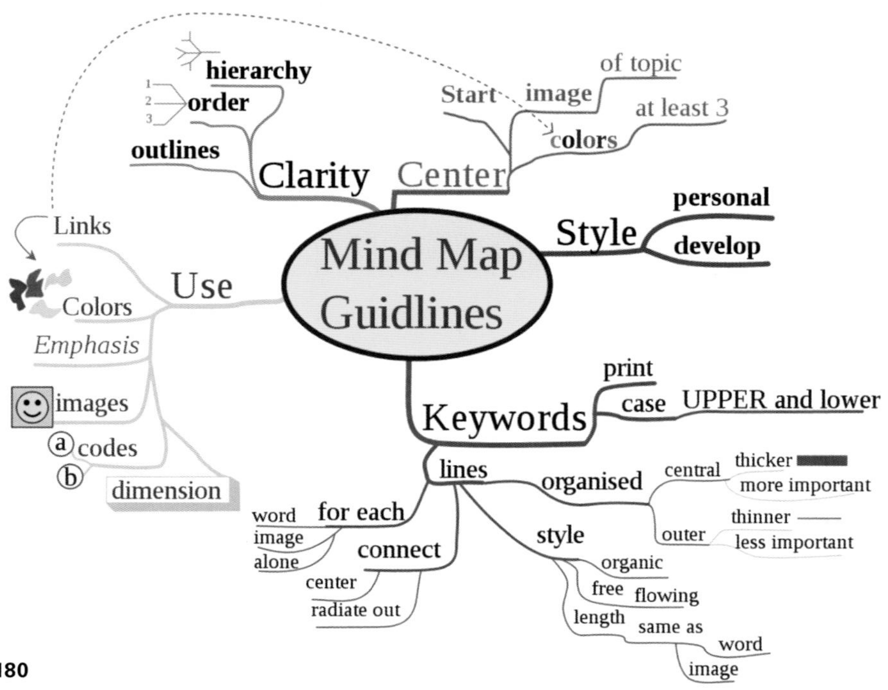

180

(58)

different modes of knowing, diff modes of sharing knowledge

learn how to understand and adopt methods of different discursive fields

rich use of historical sources of problematic within the field

Ecologies of knowledges

multiple knowledges

design studies

locus of a body of thought

design as a research community could have a name

development validation

from better use of existing knowledge shared across domains

new knowledge will arise

presentation styles

DR

standards and feedback

open ways of research

cultural ecology of events

conference like design plus research open, non-standard

conference within an established society

emerging doctoral programs, tough standards of research and argumentation (raise the bar)

Victor Margolin

For DI - Event structures and designed experience

Dewey on Event

ask citation on Gulbenkian Foundation report

181

Positioning maps

How do similar items compare in relation to two sets of opposite positions?

Positioning maps are also known as *semantic differential maps*.

Positioning maps are used to compare products, companies, political parties, and other entities according to attributes that may be difficult to quantify exactly.

Positioning maps are two-dimensional coordinate systems where each of the axes represents a semantic differential, i.e. a scale between two bipolar positions, such as high and low, contemporary and traditional, or functional and aesthetic.

A positioning map takes two chosen differential scales into consideration. Other positioning maps concerning the same subject can be constructed with other differentials. The critical point is to find the two most strategically relevant sets of contrasting qualities: what matters in the actual situation? The objectivity and exactness we otherwise strive for in information graphics may be less apparent in positioning maps. The positions typically defy exact specification; they are estimated after careful comparison with one another. The rationale is that a good estimate is better than nothing.

Before entering new markets, companies develop positioning maps to estimate the existing supply from other companies and to see if there are gaps in the market and potential demand for their products. Like other visual displays, positioning maps help the sponsor to better understand what he already knows.

Figure 182 Positioning map. Car manufacturers carefully watch the market supply on positioning maps and look out for lucrative white space. How can their existing platforms be exploited in new buyer segments? Skoda, Seat, Volkswagen, and Audi have many more cars on their positioning maps than shown here, and they probably don't use Tata Nano and Land Rover Discovery as points of reference. Also other factors than price and speed will be considered, for instance fuel economy and taxation on specific markets. The two-dimensional positioning map only takes two scales into consideration at a time. Car buyers may use similar maps to overview their options.
Source: Mads Mollerup

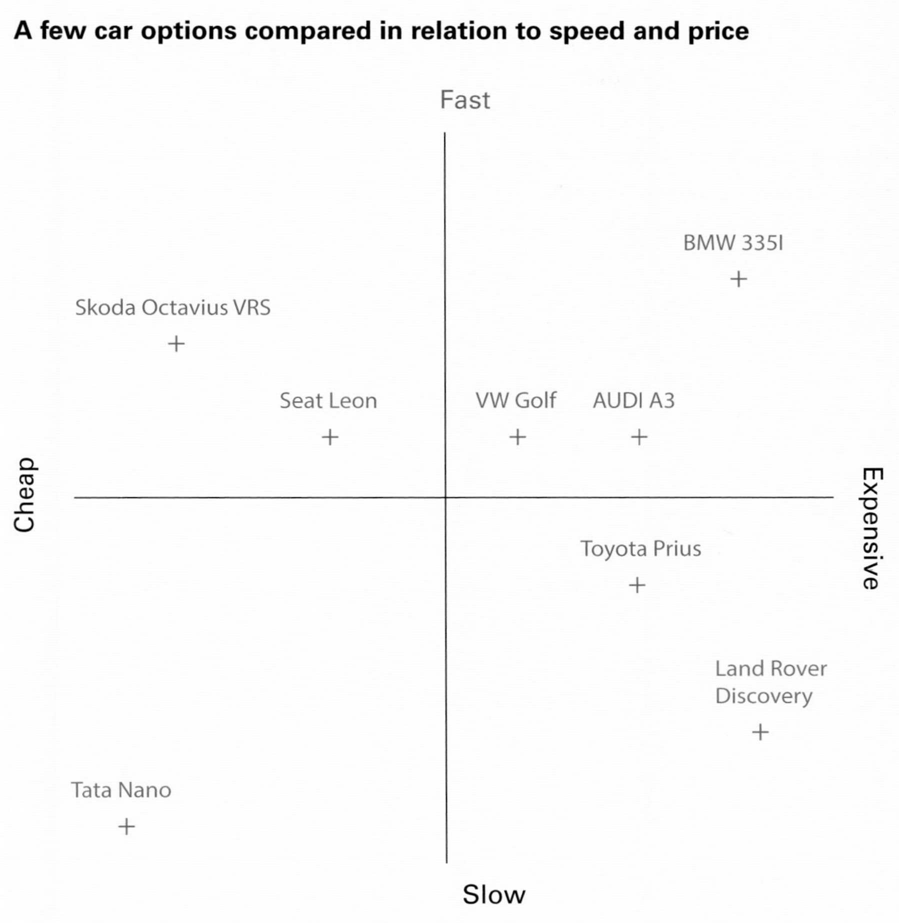
A few car options compared in relation to speed and price
Fast
BMW 335I
Skoda Octavius VRS
Seat Leon
VW Golf
AUDI A3
Cheap
Expensive
Toyota Prius
Land Rover Discovery
Tata Nano
Slow

182

Visualising connections

Timelines

When did what happen?
What happened concurrently?

Although the line has served as spatial time metaphor for several hundred years, it was not until the middle of the eighteenth century that the first graphic timeline was designed. Until then different kinds of tables had been used to visually organise historical knowledge.

Timelines have one or two functions. One function is to show the chronological development of a single phenomenon, be it the life of a famous person, an invention, a political idea, a company, or something else. The other function is to show what happened concurrently with the chronology of the subject, for example wars, political events, inventions, the lives of great artists, or natural disasters.

Graphic timelines in traditional media typically run horizontally from left to right, while timelines in digital media may run vertically up-down and demand some scrolling.

Figure 183 Timelines come in legion formats. Some are more text based than others.

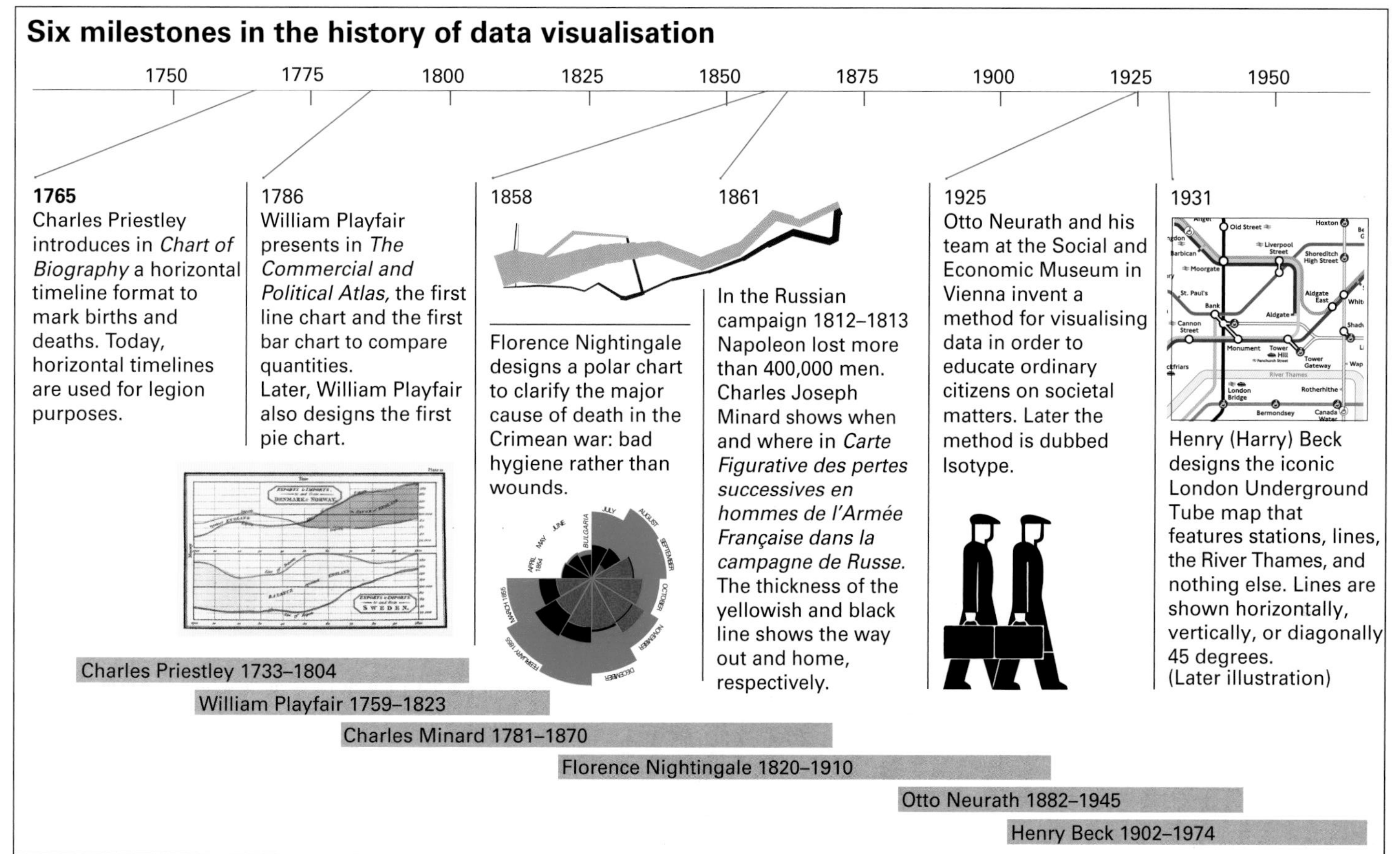

183
Six milestones in the history of data visualisation
1750
1775
1800
1825
1850
1875
1900
1925
1950
1765
Charles Priestley introduces in *Chart of Biography* a horizontal timeline format to mark births and deaths. Today, horizontal timelines are used for legion purposes.
1786
William Playfair presents in *The Commercial and Political Atlas*, the first line chart and the first bar chart to compare quantities.
Later, William Playfair also designs the first pie chart.
1858
Florence Nightingale designs a polar chart to clarify the major cause of death in the Crimean war: bad hygiene rather than wounds.
1861
In the Russian campaign 1812–1813 Napoleon lost more than 400,000 men. Charles Joseph Minard shows when and where in *Carte Figurative des pertes successives en hommes de l'Armée Française dans la campagne de Russe.* The thickness of the yellowish and black line shows the way out and home, respectively.
1925
Otto Neurath and his team at the Social and Economic Museum in Vienna invent a method for visualising data in order to educate ordinary citizens on societal matters. Later the method is dubbed Isotype.
1931
Henry (Harry) Beck designs the iconic London Underground Tube map that features stations, lines, the River Thames, and nothing else. Lines are shown horizontally, vertically, or diagonally 45 degrees.
(Later illustration)
Charles Priestley 1733–1804
William Playfair 1759–1823
Charles Minard 1781–1870
Florence Nightingale 1820–1910
Otto Neurath 1882–1945
Henry Beck 1902–1974

Flow charts

How does a process or an algorithm flow?

Flow charts describe processes and algorithms. They give overview and clarify the consecutive steps in a way that enables fast understanding.

Flow charts build on a set of generic symbols: boxes and arrows. Different trades have specialised symbols, but most flow charts can do with symbols for beginning and end (terminal), direction, action, input/output, decision, and connection with another process. Users can develop new symbols that fit special processes.

One useful application of flow charts concerns the division of a process between different workers or departments.

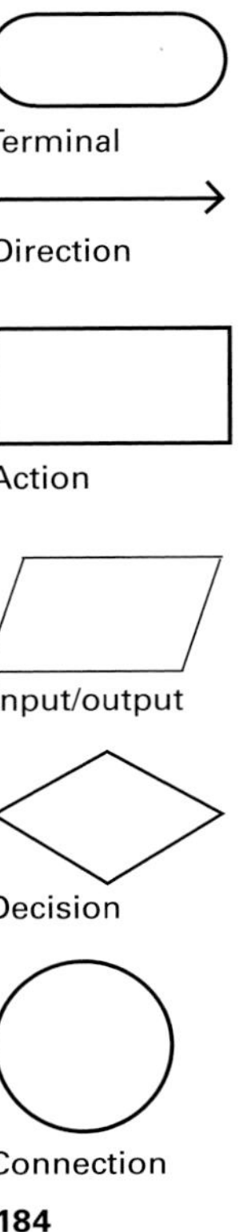

184

Figure 184 Basic flow chart symbols.

Figure 185 Flow chart describing the process of making a visual display of an already known type.

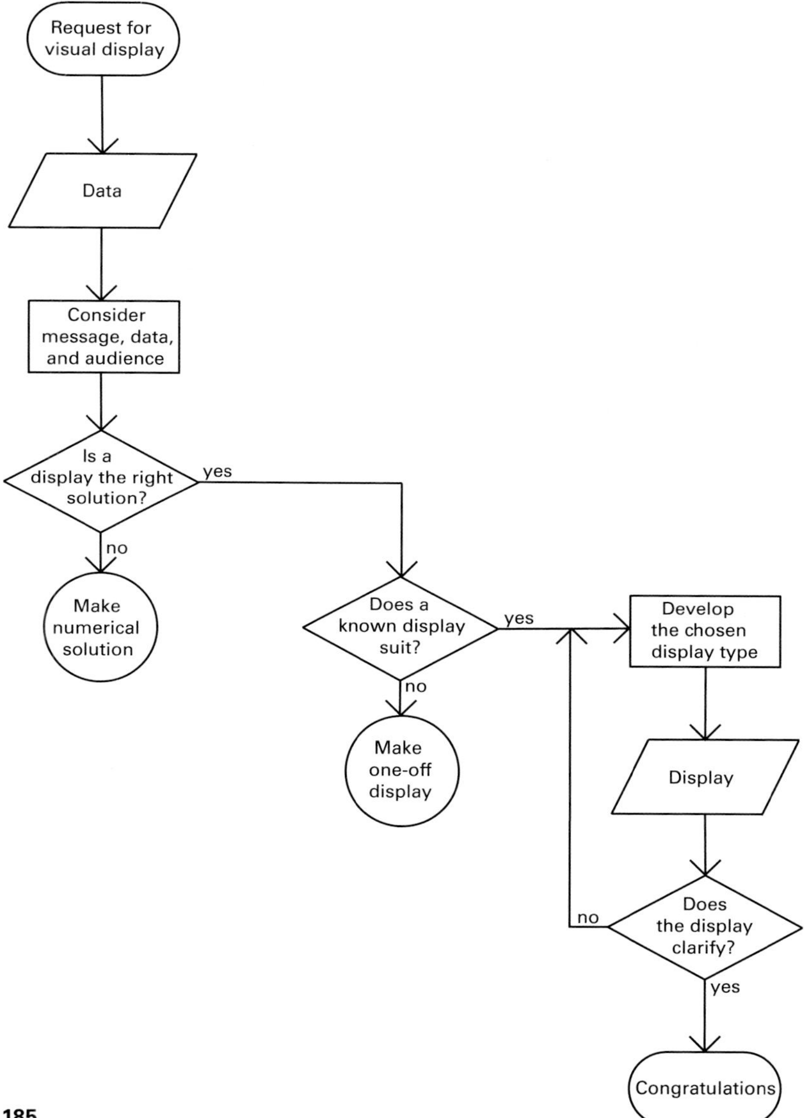
Request for visual display
Data
Consider message, data, and audience
Is a display the right solution?
yes
no
Make numerical solution
Does a known display suit?
yes
no
Make one-off display
Develop the chosen display type
Display
Does the display clarify?
no
yes
Congratulations

185

Visualising connections

Concept maps

How do the parts of a complex concept interrelate?

Concept maps, originally developed by Joseph D. Nolan in 1972, present relations in complex bodies of knowledge.

Understanding, discussion, and improvement are the obvious goals of using concept maps. Concept maps are composed of boxes and arrows and may superficially look like mind maps *(see p152)* but differ in several ways. A major difference is that concept maps allow cycles. Contrary to mind maps, concept maps allow cross-links between boxes in different segments.

Concept maps are hierarchical. They start with a central concept under exploration at the top and work downwards.

The arrows that connect boxes in concept maps are labelled with linking words or phrases such as 'results in', 'supports', 'may compromise', and 'must be coordinated with'.

Figure 186 Self-referential concept map: about concept maps.

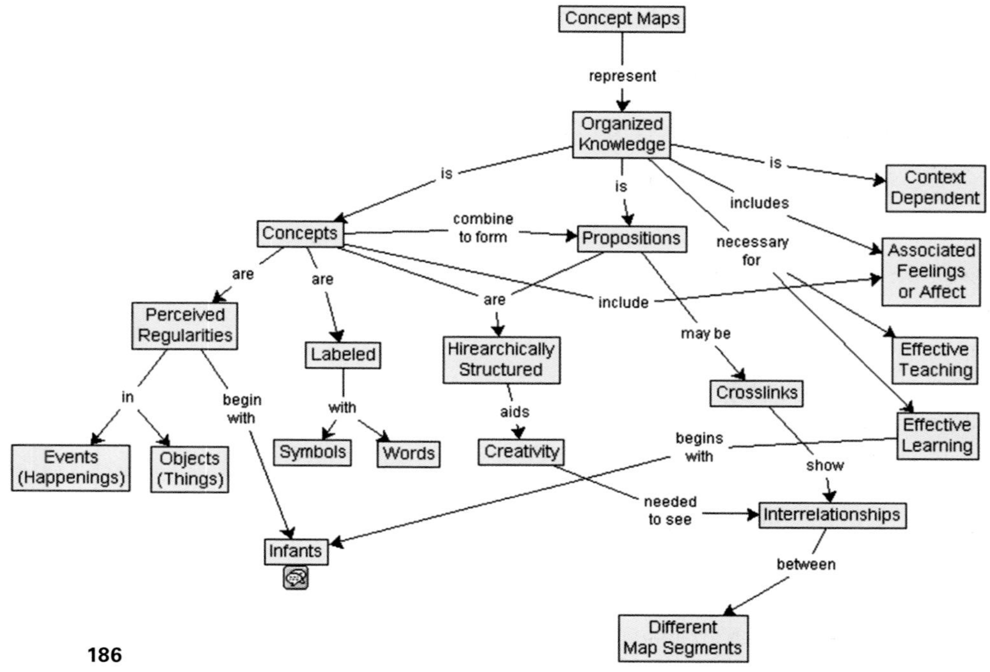
Concept Maps
represent
Organized Knowledge
is
Context Dependent
includes
Associated Feelings or Affect
is
Concepts
combine to form
Propositions
necessary for
Effective Teaching
Effective Learning
are
Perceived Regularities
are
Labeled
are
include
Hirearchically Structured
may be
Crosslinks
in
begin with
with
Events (Happenings)
Objects (Things)
Symbols
Words
aids
Creativity
begins with
show
needed to see
Interrelationships
Infants
between
Different Map Segments
186

Venn diagrams

How do different categories relate?

Venn diagrams are named after their inventor John Archibald Venn (1834–1923). They have their root in set theory, where they visualise such basic concepts as set, intersection, union, subset, superset, and set difference. Venn diagrams consist of circles, or other closed curves, that represent sets and intersect, where more than one set is present. In this way Venn diagrams visualise all possible logical relations between sets. A set can be any kind of category, object, or quality.

For graphic reasons, the number of sets must be small, typically two or three, although constructions exist with four, five, or six sets.

Figure 187 Venn diagrams showing for example the relations between two-legged animals and animals that can fly. *Union:* all two-legged animals and all animals that can fly. *Intersection:* two-legged animals that can fly (most birds and bats). *Set difference:* two-legged animals that cannot fly (for example humans and penguins) and animals with more than two legs that can fly (insects).

Figure 188 Venn diagrams with three sets are often used to illustrate situations where three demands must be met concurrently. Desirability, feasibility, and viability are the three essential concerns of design thinkers according to Tim Brown: *Change by Design*, 2009.

Figure 189 Venn diagram with four sets, perhaps more theoretically than practically interesting. Here it is used to show the possible combination of four popular movie ingredients.

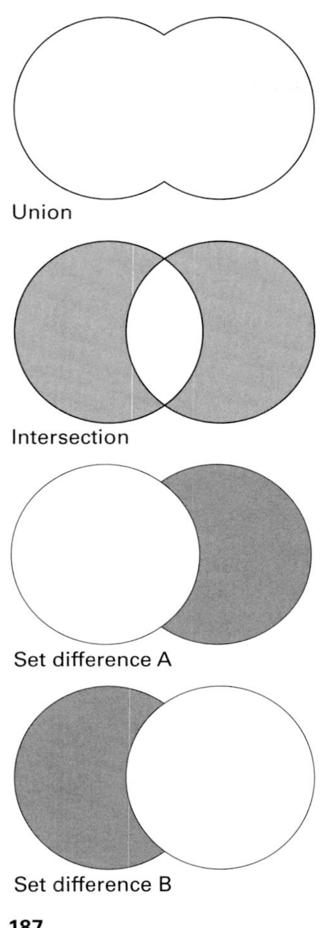

187

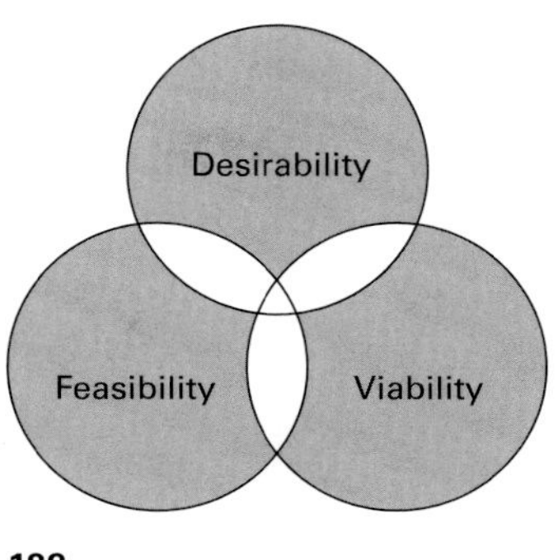

188

The making of a box office hit

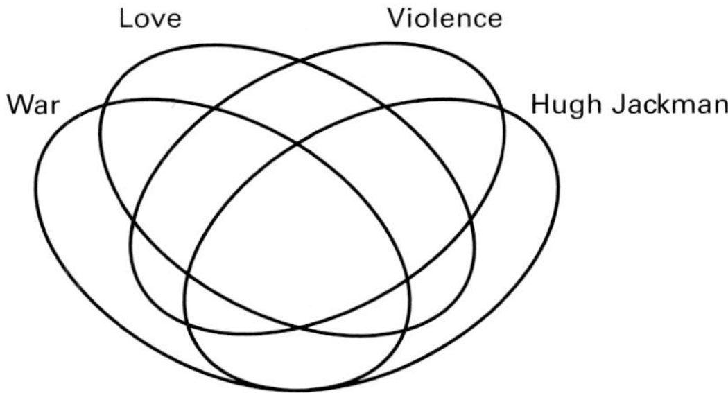

189

Carroll diagrams

How do different categories relate?

Carroll diagrams are also known as *Carroll Squares.*

Lewis Carroll, the author of *Alice in Wonderland*, alias Charles Lutwidge Dodgson (1832–1898), developed the rectangular Carroll diagram, a two-by- two matrix that represents the same type of information as a Venn diagram. Carroll diagrams are typically used with two variables, but Carroll also developed diagrams for three and more variables.

The Carroll diagram with two variables is often used by businesses notably by the Boston Consulting Group in its Growth Share Matrix that categorises a company's products according to market growth and relative market share.

	Desktop	Portable
Professional	Apple machine	Apple machine
Consumer	Apple machine	Apple machine

190

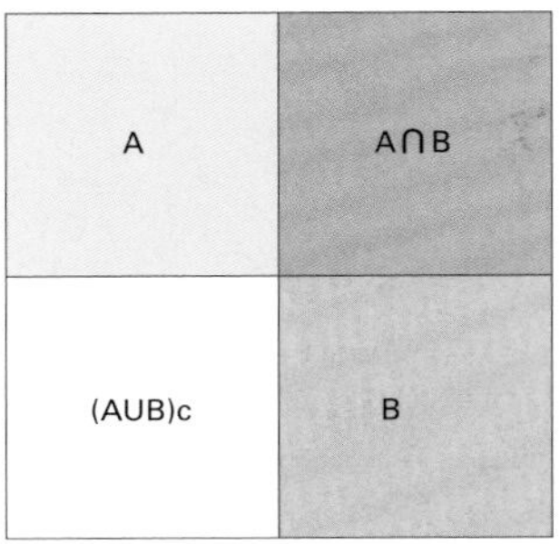

191

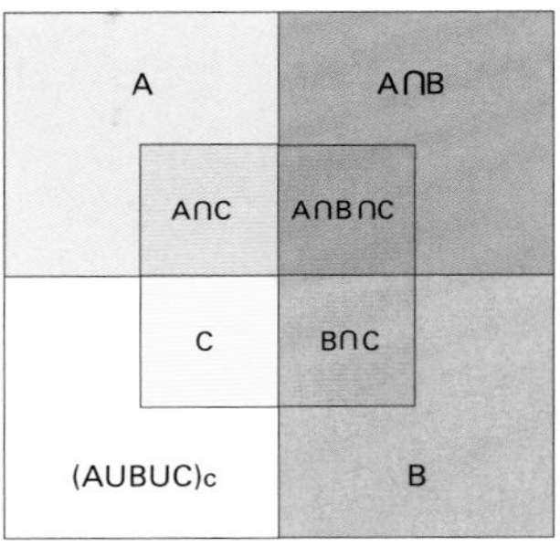

192

Figure 190 Carroll diagram showing the four product categories suggested by Steve Jobs after his return to Apple in 1997.

Figure 191 Carroll diagram with two sets showing set theory notation.
A∩B = Intersection: Objects that belong both to A and B.
(AUB)c = Complement: Objects that do not belong to A or B.

Figure 192 Carroll diagram with three sets.

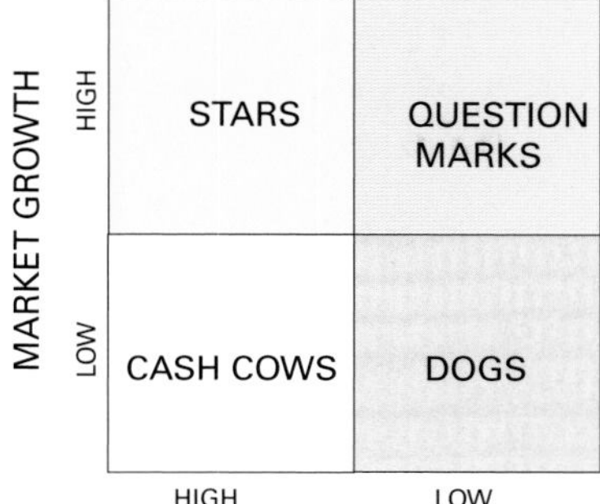

193

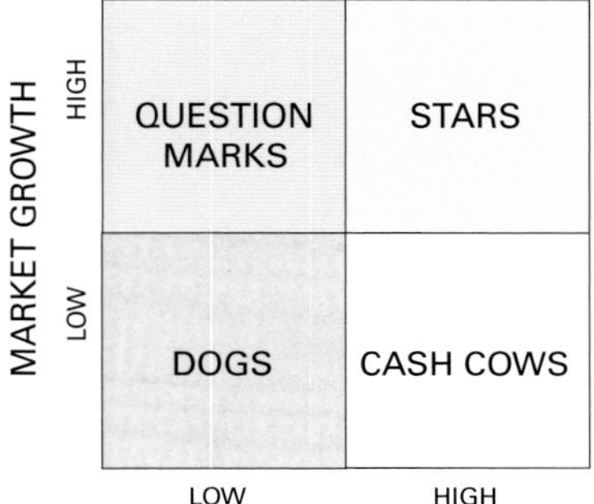

194

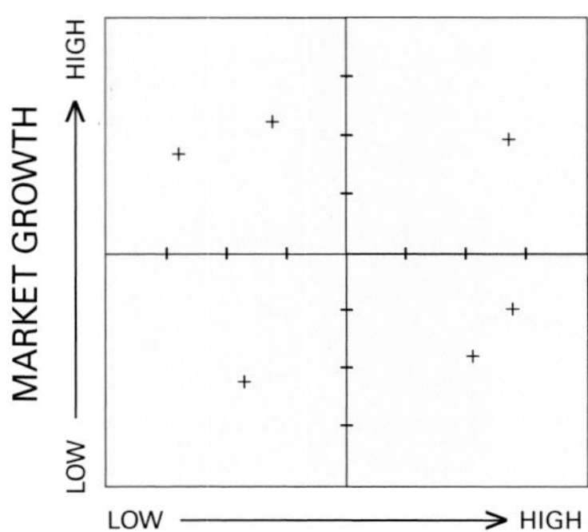

195

Figure 193 The Growth Share Matrix aka the *Boston Box* is a Carroll diagram developed by Bruce Henderson for the Boston Consulting Group. The diagram is used to analyse company units and product lines according to relative market share and growth rate. Market share indicates income. Growth rate indicates need for investment.
Cash cows have a large relative market share in a slow-growing market. Cash cows give lots of income and demand little investment. They should be milked.
Dogs have small relative market share in a slow-growing market. The future does not belong to them, unless there are special synergy effects.
Question marks have a small relative market share in a fast-growing market. They give relatively little income and demand relatively large investment. They can go either way.
Stars have relatively large market share in a fast-growing market. When the market settles they may become cash cows, or dogs.

Figure 194 The Growth Share Matrix with the x axis reversed, to let both axes run from low to high – as in a coordinate system.

Figure 195 The Growth Share Matrix can be used as a rough four box model for analysing units and activities. The analysis can be refined if the entities are more precisely located along the two axes.

Euler diagrams

How do different categories relate?

Euler diagrams were invented by mathematician Leonhard Euler (1707–1783). Like Venn diagrams, they visualise logical relations between sets. A set can be any kind of category. The difference between Venn and Euler diagrams is that Venn diagrams show all possible combinations, while Euler diagrams exclude empty combinations and only show actual combinations. In some cases this implies a considerable simplification that allows more variables.

To show the logical relations between beverages, wine, and Chablis an Euler diagram *(see figure 196)* will do with three nested circles while a Venn diagram *(see figure 197)* uses three intersecting circles showing all seven (2^3-1) possible combinations. Out of these, four are empty:

1 B and W and C
2 B and W not C
3 ~~B and C not W~~
4 B not W not C
5 ~~W and C not B~~
6 ~~W not B not C~~
7 ~~C not W not B~~

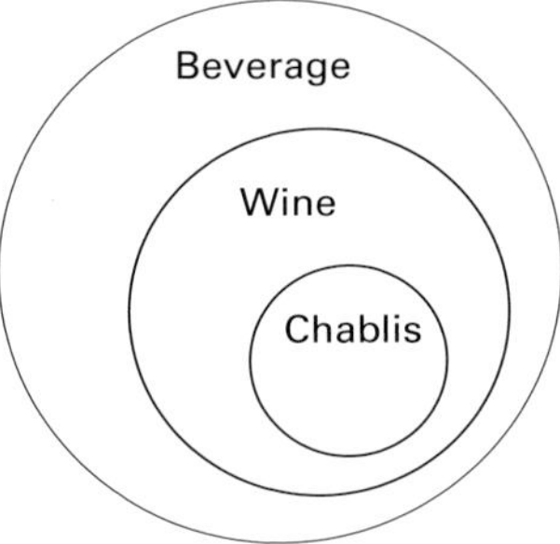

196

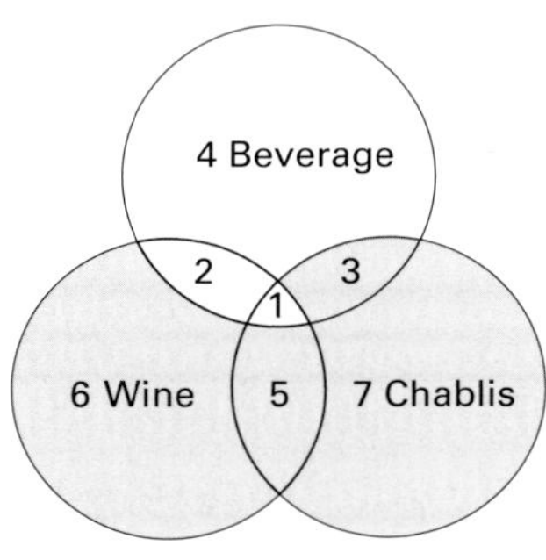

197

Figure 196 Euler diagrams only show the actual combinations of three nested categories.

Figure 197 Venn diagrams show all possible combinations of three nested categories.

Figure 198 The British Isles Eulerised.

Figure 199 Venn or Euler? In daily conversation less formal diagrams consisting of overlapping areas may work.
Design: Charles Eames for the exhibition *What is Design?* at Louvre, 1967
Source: Eames Office

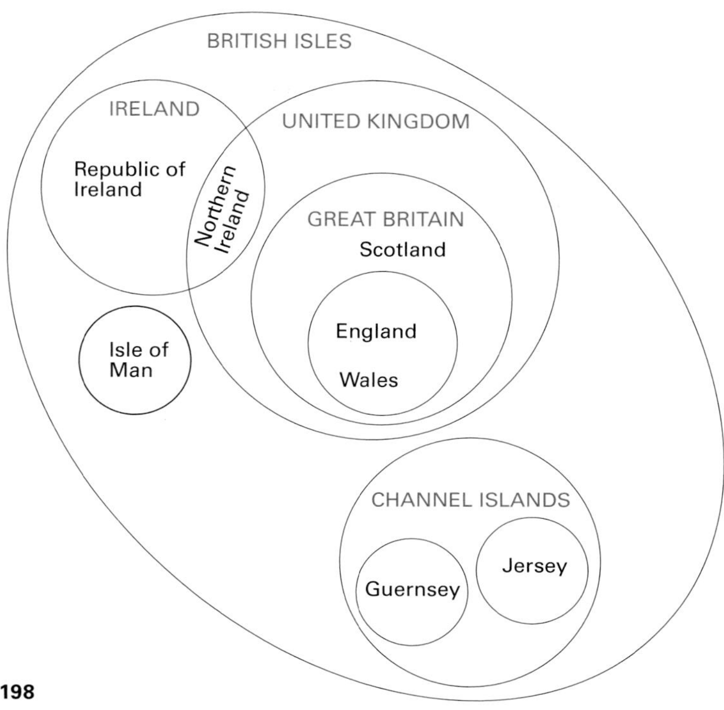
BRITISH ISLES
IRELAND
UNITED KINGDOM
Republic of Ireland
Northern Ireland
GREAT BRITAIN
Scotland
England
Wales
Isle of Man
CHANNEL ISLANDS
Guernsey
Jersey

198

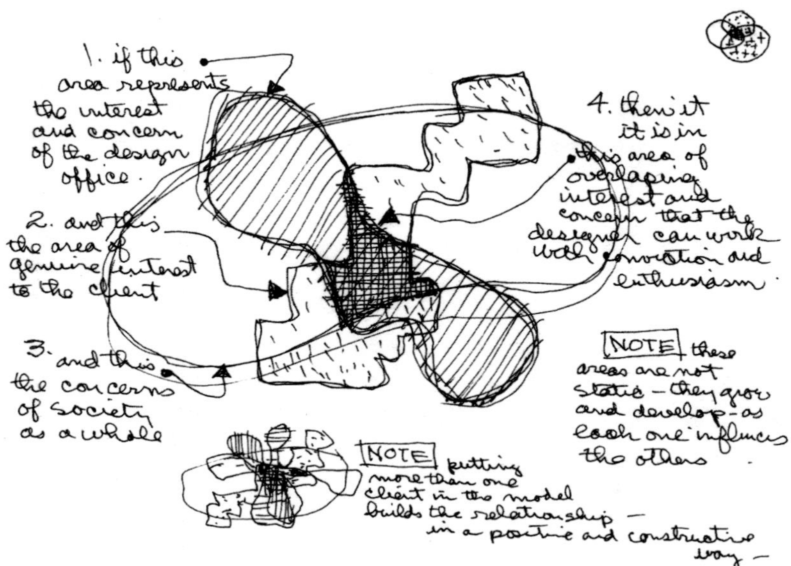
1. if this area represents the interest and concern of the design office.
2. and this the area of genuine interest to the client
3. and this the concerns of society as a whole
4. then it it is in this area of overlapping interest and concern that the designer can work with conviction and enthusiasm.
NOTE these areas are not static – they grow and develop – as each one influences the others.
NOTE putting more than one client in the model builds the relationship – in a positive and constructive way –

199

Sources

Bertin, Jaques
Semiology of Graphics
University of Wisconsin Press, Madison, WI, 1983

Brodersen, Lars
Kort som kommunikation
Forlaget Kortgruppen, Frederikshavn, 1999

Brown, Tim
Change by Design
HarperCollins, New York, NY, 2009

Buzan, Tony
The Mind Map Book
Penguin Books, 1996

Chambers, J.M., Cleveland, W.S., Kleiner, B., & Tukey, P.A.
Graphic Methods for Data Analysis
Wadsworth, Belmont, CA, 1983

Cleveland, W.S.
The Elements of Graphing Data
Wadsworth, Monterey, CA, 1985

Garland, Ken
Mr. Beck's Underground Map
Capital Transport Publishing, Harrow Weald, 1994

Guiraud, Pierre
Semiology
Routledge, London, 1975

Kosslyn, Stephen M.
Graph Design for the Eye and Mind
Oxford University Press, New York, NY, 2006

Lidwell, W., Holden, K., & Butler, J.
Universal Principles of Design
Rockport, Beverly, MA, 2003

Monmonier, Mark
How to Lie with Maps
University of Chicago Press, Chicago, IL, 1991

Neurath, Otto
From hieroglyphics to Isotype: A visual autobiography
Hyphen Press, London, 2010

Ovenden, Mark
Paris Underground
Penguin Books, London, 2009

Ovenden, Mark
Railway Maps of the World
Viking, New York, 2011

Ovenden, Mark
Transit Maps of the World
Penguin Books, London, 2007

Playfair, William
The Commercial and Political Atlas and Statistical Breviary
Cambridge University Press, Cambridge, 2005

Rosenberg, Daniel & Grafton, Anthony
Cartographies of Time: A history of the timeline
Princeton Architectural Press, New York, NY, 1966

Sims-Knight, Judith E.
To Picture or Not to Picture: How to decide
Visible Language, Volume 26, Numbers 3 and 4, 1992

Sources

Tufte, Edward R.
Beautiful Evidence
Graphics Press, Cheshire, CT, 2006

Tufte, Edward, R.
Envisioning Information
Graphics Press, Cheshire, CT, 1990

Tufte, Edward R.
The Visual Display of Quantitative Information
Graphics Press, Cheshire, CT, 1983, 2001

Tufte, Edward R.
Visual Explanations
Graphics Press, Cheshire, CT, 1997

The Guardian DataBlog
www.theguardian.com/news/datablog

Information Design Journal
www.ingentaconnect.com/content/jbp/idj

Parsons Journal of Information Mapping
http//pjim.newschool.edu.

Index

Acknowledgements

This book would not have become this book without the valuable help of friends, colleagues, and the sponsors of good design.

University Distinguished Professor Ken Friedman polished the language and offered editorial advice.

Professor Alan Whitfield read the manuscript, offering comments and advice on quantitative displays.

Dr Katherine Hepworth assisted on several levels as my research assistant.

Lecturer Andrew Kean assisted in preparation of the book for printing.

Designers Nina Kampmann and Niels Kierkegaard offered advice on using graphic software.

Designers and companies from around the world contributed visual displays.

I alone am to blame for errors, great or small.

Per Mollerup

Per Mollerup, Dr.Tech., is Professor of Communication Design at Swinburne University of Technology, School of Design, Melbourne.
From 1984 to 2009 Per Mollerup was the owner and principal of Designlab in Copenhagen, an award-winning Danish design consultancy specialising in wayshowing and branding. Clients included airports, transportation companies, hospitals, museums, and private companies.

www.permollerup.com

Other books by Per Mollerup include:

Marks of Excellence: The history and taxonomy of trademarks, 1997, 2013.

Collapsibles: A design album of space-saving objects, 2002.

Wayshowing: A guide to environmental signage, 2005.

Brandbook: Branding, feelings, reason, 2008 (in Danish).

PowerNotes: Slide presentations reconsidered, 2011. Downloadable from http://hdl.handle.net/1959.3/191214

Wayshowing>Wayfinding: Basic & interactive, 2013 (revised and expanded version of *Wayshowing: A guide to environmental signage*, 2005).